cooking with mushrooms

cooking with mushrooms

STEVEN WHEELER

LORENZ BOOKS

PUBLISHERS NOTE

The publishers and authors cannot accept responsibility for any identification of any mushroom made by the users of this guide. Although many species are edible for many people, some species cause allergic reactions or illness to some people: these are totally unpredictable. Therefore, the publishers and authors cannot take responsibility for any effects from eating any wild mushroom.

This edition published by Lorenz Books
an imprint of
Anness Publishing Limited
Hermes House, 88-89 Blackfriars Road
London SE1 8HA

This edition distributed in Canada by Raincoast Books
8680 Cambie Street, Vancouver, British Columbia V6P 6M9

ISBN 0-7548-0306-6

A CIP catalogue record for this book is available from the British Library

Publisher: Joanna Lorenz
Senior Editor: Clare Nicholson
Designer: Michael Morey
Photography: James Duncan

Front Cover: William Lingwood, Photographer;
Helen Trent, Stylist; Sunil Vijayakar, Home Economist

Also published as part of a larger compendium,
The Ultimate Mushroom Book

Printed and bound in Hong Kong/China

1 3 5 7 9 10 8 6 4 2

NOTE

For all recipes, quantities are given in both metric and imperial measures and, where appropriate, measures are also given in standard cups and spoons. Follow one set, but not a mixture because they are not interchangeable.

Standard spoon and cup measures are level.
1 tbsp = 15 ml, 1 tsp = 5 ml, 1 cup = 250 ml/8 fl oz

Medium eggs should be used unless otherwise stated

Contents

Introduction

From the cook's point of view, wild mushrooms are an irresistible source of flavour, texture and aroma. The recipes in this book explore the qualities of over thirty types of edible mushrooms and will show you how best to cook and enjoy them.

The passions associated with picking mushrooms are easily aroused when we realize how many good mushrooms there are growing freely in our woods and fields. Coupled with the excitement of picking mushrooms in the wild is the risk of handling poisonous varieties, such as the death cap *Amanita phalloides*, panther cap *Amanita pantherina*, yellow stainer *Agaricus xanthodermus* and destroying angel *Amanita virosa*. These often deadly poisonous mushrooms can easily be mistaken for the common and edible field mushroom *Agaricus campestris*. For your own safety, never touch a mushroom you cannot identify. When possible, accompany someone who knows which mushrooms are safe, and remember, if in doubt, don't touch them.

There are over a thousand varieties of mushroom known to be edible. The mushrooms which are best to eat are a question of taste, but it is generally agreed that the finest include the cep *Boletus edulis*, bay boletus *Boletus badius*, morel *Morchella esculenta*, chanterelle *Cantharellus cibarius* and chicken of the woods, *Laetiporus sulphureus*. These mushrooms fetch a high price at market and are sold mainly to the restaurant trade. Occasionally you may find them for sale in specialist food stores. Most precious of all is the fresh truffle which is found mainly in northern Italy and southern parts of France. Black and white truffles are found beneath the soil in mature woodland and are prized for their mysterious scent which, it is said, imitates the pheromone that cause pigs to mate.

The scent of wild mushrooms in damp woodland is enough to get most people on their knees scratching through the undergrowth. You may not be lucky enough to find a truffle, but there are many fine mushrooms to find and a home-cooked breakfast is a welcome return for the hungry mushroom picker. Even if you've only managed to find a few mushrooms, they will go a long way to flavour a plate of scrambled eggs. Parsley, thyme and fennel-scented chervil bring out their flavour as will a splash of sherry. Later in the day, wild mushrooms are ideal cooked in warming soups and broths. More delicate mushrooms are better suited to light broths.

Poultry and game taste good with mushroom flavours, either roasted, braised or sautéed. When cooking free-range chicken, try the delicate richness of the chanterelle, saffron milk-cap *Lactarius deliciosus*, hedgehog fungus *Hydnum repandum* and St George's mushroom *Calocybe gambosa*. Guinea fowl and pheasant carry the robust flavour of the fresh or dried cep, bay boletus, parasol mushroom and blewit. Wild duck mirrors the smoky richness of the morel and is good served with a glass of Madeira. Chicken of the woods has such a convincing taste, texture and appearance that it can be used as a substitute for chicken in chicken recipes.

Beef is a perfect match for the open field, horse and parasol mushroom. Cooked slowly with red wine, onions and a good stock, they are the making of a fine beef stew, rich and round with a luscious mushroom gravy. The delicate quality of lamb allies with the apricot sweetness of the chanterelle and saffron milk-cap. Pork belongs in a slow pot with a sauce of Jeruselem artichokes, horn of plenty *Craterellus cornucopiodes* and a purée of green olives.

The flavour of wild mushrooms is most effective with other wild foods. The sea is perhaps the most bountiful source of wild food, both fish and shellfish. Providing they are fresh (and in some cases alive), fish and shellfish are ideal ingredients to accompany a selection of wild mushrooms. When you have chosen the finest ingredients, simplicity is the best course of action, with particular care given to the preparation of sauces and garnishes. As a rule, if the fish has a delicate flavour, select a sweeter, subtle-tasting mushroom. Flat fish, such as sole, plaice and turbot suit closed field varieties with a little parsley, lemon and thyme. Stronger oily fish such as salmon, tuna and trout benefit from the assertive quality of the cep, bay boletus, shiitake, and blewit.

Wild mushrooms have been valued for centuries as an alternative to meat; a delight for those who know how and where to pick them. Meat has always been expensive at market and mushrooms have long been used make it go further. Presently, with eating habits veering away from meat for health reasons, vegetarians are discovering again the value of wild mushrooms for their first rate flavour, texture and goodness. Mushrooms contain essential minerals potassium, magnesium and iron. They are high in niacin and contain other B group vitamins. Mushrooms consist of 2–8% protein and contain around 35 calories per 100 g (4 oz).

GOOD EDIBLE MUSHROOMS

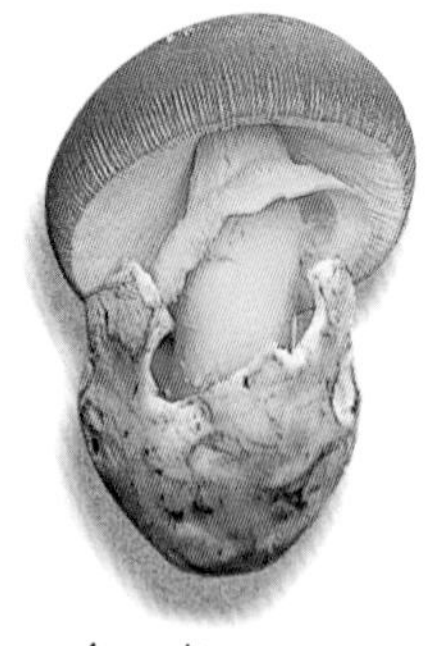

Amanita caesarea
Caesar's mushroom

Armillaria mellea
Honey fungus

Boletus edulis
Cep

Cantharellus cibarius
Chanterelle

Agaricus campestris and *bisporus*
Field mushroom

Boletus badius
Bay boletus

Calocybe gambosa
St George's mushroom

The assessment and value of edible mushrooms is open to opinion. Apart from the principle of putting delicate mushrooms with subtle foods and not putting mushrooms that stain black in creamy sauces, there are no rules to follow. Below is a brief and personal assessment of good edible mushrooms.

Agaricus campestris and *bisporus*
Field Mushroom
Open and closed field mushrooms provide a well-known flavour to everyday cooking. Take care when picking not to confuse this common mushroom with the poisonous yellow stainer *Agaricus xanthodermus*, destroying angel *Amanita virosa* and spring amanita *Amanita verna*.

Amanita caesarea
Caesar's Mushroom
The Caesar's mushroom is valued for its sweet chestnut quality. It has a russet orange to yellow glow. It is not found in Britain. Young specimens are best eaten raw in salads.

Armillaria mellea
Honey Fungus or Boot-lace Fungus
This fungus has a strong, often astringent, smell. It is edible only after blanching in water which must be discarded. However, after blanching, honey fungus softens and loses much of its appeal. It is an acquired taste.

Boletus badius
Bay Boletus
The bay boletus shares many qualities with the cep. Young specimens are particularly good and offer a lingering richness to be enjoyed raw in salads or cooked simply to respect their flavour.

Boletus edulis
Cep or Penny Bun
The cep is considered best when small and tight. Good specimens are heavy for their size and have an almost leafy, richness when eaten raw. Larger ceps are best cooked in butter with a few herbs. Another bolete which is popular and looks like the cep is *Boletus pruinatus*.

Calocybe gambosa
St George's Mushroom
The St George's mushroom has a rich meaty scent and a nutty flavour when cooked. They are good eaten raw or with a touch of garlic and a few chives in an olive oil dressing.

Cantharellus cibarius
Chanterelle
The intensely orange trumpet shape of the chanterelle has an appealing scent of dried apricots with a hint of

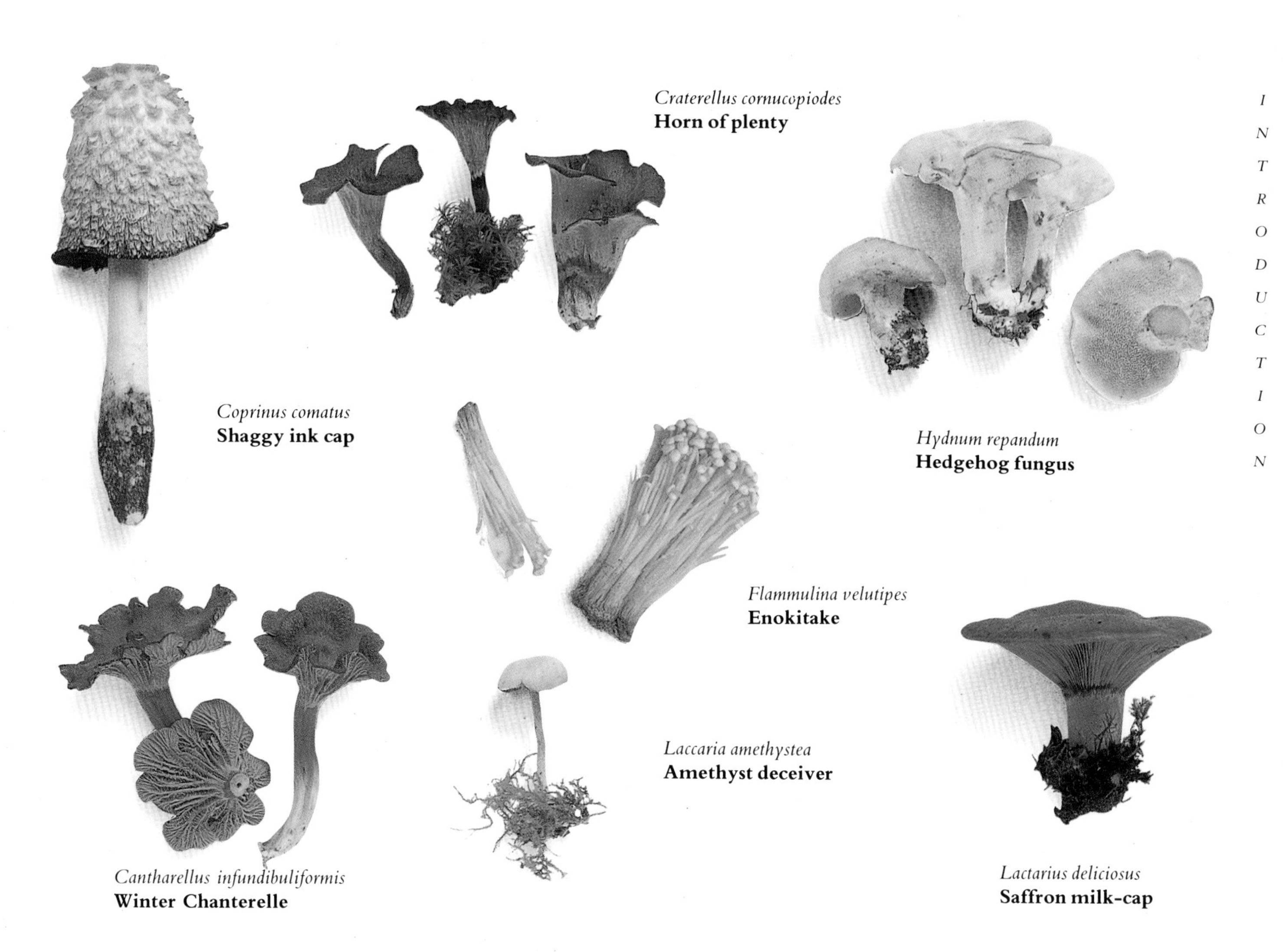

Craterellus cornucopiodes
Horn of plenty

Coprinus comatus
Shaggy ink cap

Hydnum repandum
Hedgehog fungus

Flammulina velutipes
Enokitake

Laccaria amethystea
Amethyst deceiver

Cantharellus infundibuliformis
Winter Chanterelle

Lactarius deliciosus
Saffron milk-cap

citrus. Chanterelle are best tossed in nut brown butter, although their colour and flavour remain true even after slow cooking. It is essential to avoid the false chanterelle *Hygrophoropsis aurantiaca* which can cause alarming hallucinations.

Cantharellus infundibuliformis
Winter Chanterelle
This mushroom has a rich mossy scent that combines well with other mushrooms. After trimming at the base, the winter chanterelle is best used whole.

Coprinus comatus
Shaggy Ink Cap or Lawyer's Wig
The shaggy ink cap has a delicate flavour not unlike the field mushroom. Pick young specimens that have yet to blacken and deteriorate around the fringe. Use in smooth soups and sauces. Do not use the common ink cap *Coprinus atramentarius*; this causes a violent reaction when consumed with alcohol.

Craterellus cornucopiodes
Horn of Plenty or Trompette des Morts
The horn of plenty has a sweet earthy richness that goes a long way to flavour soups, stews and casseroles. Its jet black appearance does not bleed, even after lengthy cooking.

Flammulina velutipes
Enokitake
These long-stemmed pinhead mushrooms are grown commercially on the stumps of the enoki or Chinese hackberry tree. They have a delicate flavour reminiscent of white pepper and lemon. Serve them raw or cooked in a light broth. Enokitake are available in Oriental grocers.

Hydnum repandum
Hedgehog Fungus or Pied de Mouton
Young hedgehog fungus has a peppery watercress quality that is appreciated raw in salads. Mature specimens can be bitter and are best cooked with sweet butter and herbs.

Laccaria amethystea
Amethyst Deceiver
These distinctive grape coloured mushrooms have a subtle, gentle flavour, but provide colour and interest when put with paler mushrooms.

Lactarius deliciosus
Saffron Milk-cap
The saffron milk-cap is prized for its saffron orange colour and firm texture. It has little flavour. Mature specimens often harbour insect larvae in the stem and centre cap, so take care when selecting.

Laetiporus sulphureus
Chicken of the woods

Leccinum versipelle
Orange birch bolete

Marasmius oreades
Fairy ring champignon

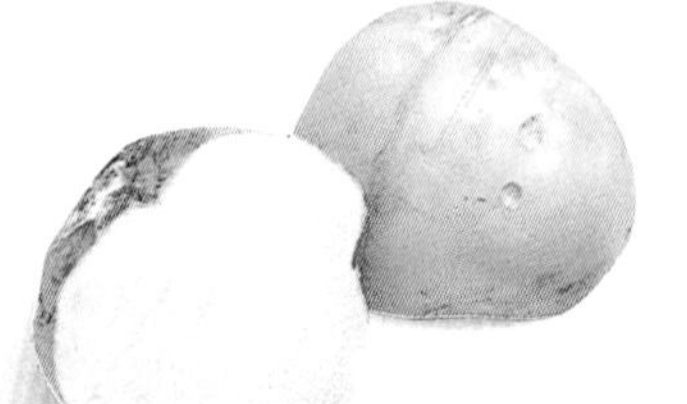

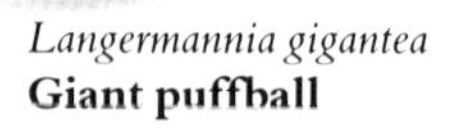

Langermannia gigantea
Giant puffball

Macrolepiota procera
Parasol mushroom

Lentinus edodes
Shiitake

Lepista nuda
Wood blewit

Lepista saeva
Field blewit

Morchella esculenta and *elata*
Morels

Laetiporus sulphureus

Chicken of the Woods or Sulphur Polypore

Chicken of the woods has an intriguing flavour and texture of roast chicken. When fresh, moist and fragrant, the fungus can be used to replace chicken in many recipes.

Langermannia gigantea

Giant Puffball

When sliced open, the young giant puffball has a gentle meaty rich aroma similar in some ways to the cep. Older specimens discolour yellow when cut and should not be eaten.

Leccinum versipelle

Orange Birch Bolete

An attractive mushroom with a freckled mud-spattered stem. It has a tawny orange cap which fades with age. It softens when cooked and provides a good texture for soups and casseroles.

Lentinus edodes

Shiitake

Shiitake are grown commercially in the Far East on logs that are taken from the oak related *shii* tree. They have a robust beefy sweetness that remains even after lengthy cooking.

Lepista nuda (syn. *Tricholoma nuda*) and *Lepista saeva*

The Wood and Field Blewit

Both field and wood blewits have an assertive pine-rich perfume, that belongs with the pronounced flavour of game, toasted nuts and cheeses.

Macrolepiota procera

Parasol Mushroom

This handsome mushroom stands proudly on a tough inedible stem. Its cap offers a gamey rich flavour which strengthens when mature. Parasol mushrooms are best sautéed in butter with a few fresh herbs.

Marasmius oreades

Fairy Ring Champignon

One of the first mushrooms to appear in spring, the fairy ring champignon tastes just as good as it looks. Fresh and dried, this common mushroom has an oaky scent which is best cooked simply in sweet butter. Great care should be taken not to confuse the fairy ring champignon with the deadly poisonous *Clitocybe rivulosa.*

Morchella esculenta, vulgaris and *elata*

Morels

The morels are the most exciting springtime fungi. Both fresh and dried morels are prized for their tobacco-rich scent of sulphur and oak. This curious scent combines especially well with eggs, beef and game. A splash of Madeira will promote their flavour.

Pleurotus ostreatus
Oyster mushroom

Pleurotus citrinopileatus
Yellow oyster mushroom

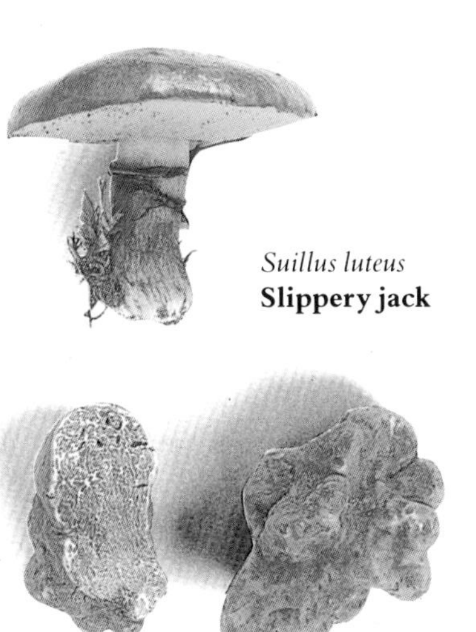

Suillus luteus
Slippery jack

Tuber magnatum
White truffle

Russula cyanoxantha
Charcoal burner

Sparassis crispa
Cauliflower fungus

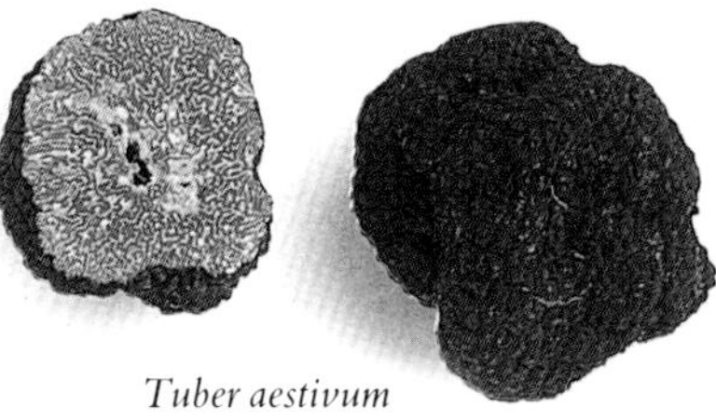

Tuber aestivum
Summer truffle

Pleurotus citrinopileatus
Yellow Oyster Mushroom
This pretty mushroom is designed by the mushroom cultivator to capture our attention in the supermarket. However, it tastes of very little and its colour disappears when cooked.

Pleurotus ostreatus
Oyster Mushroom
Both wild and cultivated oyster mushrooms have little flavour or aroma. Young specimens are best and provide good bulk when combining with stronger flavoured mushrooms.

Russula cyanoxantha
Charcoal Burner
The charcoal burner is an excellent mushroom to eat. However, it is a member of a very large genus and identification within the group can be very difficult. Correct identification is essential.

Sparassis crispa
Cauliflower Fungus
The cauliflower fungus is known more for its texture than its flavour. When raw and dried it has a curious scent of latex and ammonia which goes after brief cooking. The crisp texture of cauliflower fungus is appreciated when combined with other mushrooms.

Suillus luteus (syn. *Boletus luteus*)
Slippery Jack Pine Bolete or Sticky Bun
The slippery jack, so named because of its gluten covered cap, tends to absorb moisture in wet weather. When cooked, it softens to provide a basis for smooth soups and sauces.

Tuber aestivum
Summer Truffle
Less intensely flavoured than the white truffle, this warty black variety has a more delicate aroma associated with oak woodlands rather than the farm. More robust in texture than its white counterpart, the summer truffle should be pared before slicing raw. Truffles benefit from a few drops of truffle oil added towards the end of cooking.

Tuber magnatum
Piedmont or White Truffle
This rare and expensive tuber is found in very limited areas, mostly in northern Italy. It has a strong and curious aroma connected with the intensity of a pig sty! To touch, the white truffle has the fragility of firm fresh yeast. Unfortunately highly trained dogs or pigs are needed to find it. If you are fortunate enough to come by a white truffle, scrub it clean and shave over plainly cooked food. The flavour of the white truffle goes if it is cooked.

Drying Mushrooms

The process of drying mushrooms intensifies individual flavours and aromas. The cep develops a prolonged beefy rich aroma with a chamois leather sweetness. The bay boletus have a more pronounced sweetness and a less complex aroma. The morel develops a sulphur-rich, beefy, almost smoky quality, while fairy rings have a gentle sweetness. The cauliflower fungus has a strong latex vinegar smell which disappears with cooking. The saffron milk-cap and chanterelle have a fruity richness and the horn of plenty has a dark sweet woodland flavour.

When fully dried, mushrooms will keep through the winter in air-tight jars, providing a useful and nutritious source of flavour for soups, stews and casseroles.

1 To make sure the mushrooms are free from infestation, wipe them with a damp cloth, but avoid washing and cut away damaged parts. Slice the mushrooms thinly. When drying chanterelles, remove the stems of small specimens as they tend to toughen.

2 Lay the mushrooms on a basket tray, or baking sheet lined with several layers of newspaper and a final layer of baking parchment. Put in a warm and well-ventilated place for two days. For fast drying, preheat a fan oven to 80°C/150°F/Gas low, keep the door ajar and dry the mushrooms for 2 hours. If you have a small quantity of mushrooms, consider drying them on a needle and thread.

3 *(Right)* When mushrooms are completely dry, place each variety in an air-tight jar, label and store in a dark place. If mushrooms are not fully dry before storing, moulds will grow and spoil your work.

Mushroom Powder

The intense flavour of dried mushrooms can be used in powder form to enliven winter soups, stews and curries. The curry-scented milk-cap, *Lactarius camphoratus*, offers a pungent reminder of fenugreek and should always be used sparingly. The aniseed toadstool, *Clitocybe odora* is another powerful substitute for spices and can be used in sweet and savoury cooking. Other mushrooms suitable for powdering include many of the boletes and field and horse mushrooms.

1 Wipe clean the inside of a coffee grinder with a dry cloth. Put in the well-dried mushrooms and reduce to a fine powder.

2 Transfer to an air-tight jar, label and keep in a dark place. Use sparingly.

To Reconstitute Dried Mushrooms

To bring dried mushrooms back to life, they need to be soaked in warm water for 20 minutes. Boiling water will make them tough. The water used to soak dried mushrooms should be saved and added to stocks.

1 Place the mushrooms in a bowl. Cover with warm water and leave for 20 minutes.

Salt Preserving

Salt preserving is an age-old method of keeping mushrooms, and is still used in countries of the former Soviet Union. The method eliminates bacterial growth by packing mushrooms with layers of salt. The salt draws out the moisture in the mushrooms, forming a brine. Before using, the mushrooms need to be soaked in plenty of cold water to reduce saltiness. After soaking, salt preserved mushrooms can be added to braised meats such as beef, pork and tripe.

Suitable mushrooms for salting include: hedgehog fungus, oyster mushroom, bay boletus, winter chanterelle, saffron milk-cap, field and wood blewit.

The proportion of salt to mushrooms is 3–1.

1 *(Right)* Wipe the mushrooms clean with a damp cloth, trim and ensure that they are free from grit and infestation. Slice the mushrooms thickly with a stainless steel knife. Place a layer of rock or sea salt in the bottom of a covered glass or stoneware jar, layer with mushrooms. Alternate with more salt and mushrooms until full.

2 After 3–4 hours, you will find the volume of mushrooms will drop as the salt draws out their moisture. At this stage additional layers of salt and mushrooms can be added. Salted mushrooms will keep safely in a cool place for up to 12 months.

Freezing Mushrooms

To preserve mushrooms quickly and effectively, consider freezing them. Firmer varieties are best, such as shiitake, blewits, horn of plenty, chanterelle, closed field and horse mushrooms. To thaw, take Antonio Carluccio's advice and immerse briefly in boiling water before using.

1 Bring a saucepan of salted water to the boil and line a tray with greaseproof paper. Ensure mushrooms are free from grit and infestation then trim and slice thickly if large. Drop the mushrooms into the boiling water and simmer for 1 minute.

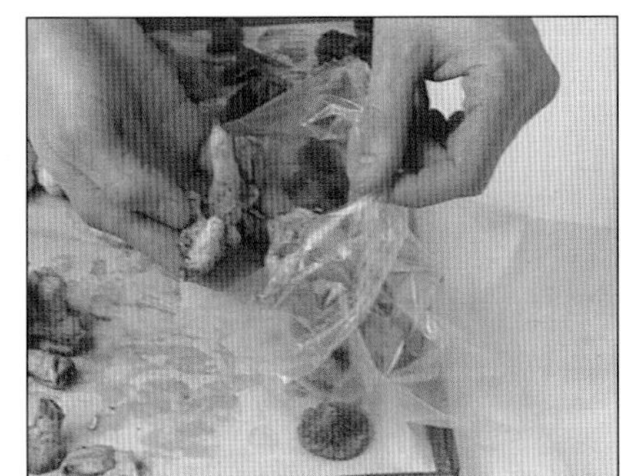

2 Drain well and open freeze for 30–40 minutes on a paper-lined tray. When frozen, turn loosely into plastic bags, label and return to the freezer for up to 6 months.

Preserving Mushrooms in Butter

Capturing the flavour and aroma of wild mushrooms in butter is a favourite method of preserving. The finest *Boletus, edulis, badius* and *pruinatus*, retain their qualities best of all when softened and combined with unsalted butter. If you are lucky enough to chance upon a few fresh truffles, these also keep well, peeled, chopped and concealed raw in butter. Other mushrooms that keep well in butter include the morel, chanterelle, saffron milk-cap and Caesar's mushroom. Wild mushroom butter is delicious melted over simply cooked meat or fish. It is also good over pasta, or with soups, sauces and gravies.

450 g / 1 lb mushrooms

175 g / 6 oz / 3/4 cup unsalted butter

15 g / 1/2 oz fresh black or white truffle, peeled and chopped (optional), or 3 drops truffle oil (optional)

1 Ensure the mushrooms are free from grit and infestation. Trim, slice and chop. Melt 50 g / 2 oz of the butter in a large non-stick frying pan. Add the mushrooms and soften over a gentle heat to reduce volume, then simmer in their own juices for 2–3 minutes. Cool.

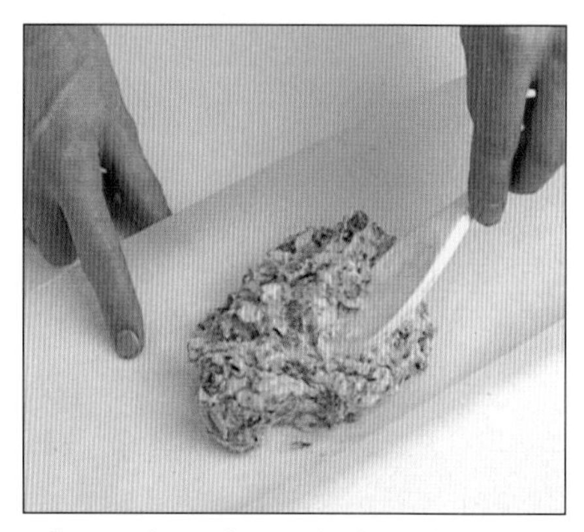

2 Combine the cooked mushrooms and truffles, or oil if you are using this instead, with the remaining butter and spoon the mixture onto a square of greaseproof paper.

3 *(Right)* Roll into a cigar shape, twist each end and label. Refrigerate for up to 10 days or freeze for up to 8 weeks.

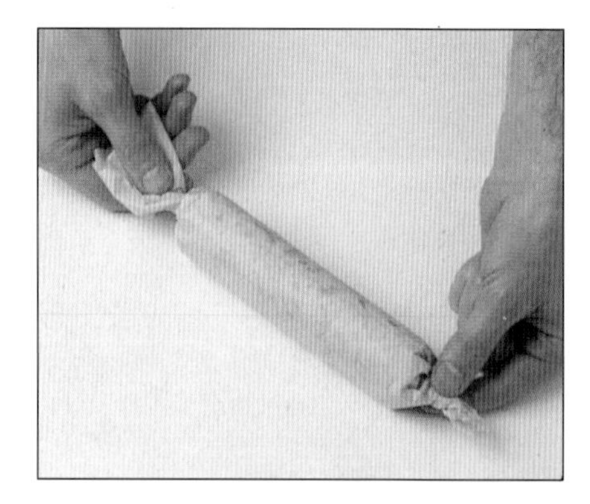

Duxelle

Duxelle is a preparation known to classical French cooking. It consists of finely chopped mushrooms and shallots cooked in butter, wine and herbs, and forms the basis for many well-known soups, sauces, stuffings, gratins and fillings. The name, according to Larousse, derives from a small town in the north east of France called Uxel. The preparation may be credited to La Varenne who cooked for the household of the Marquis d'Uxelles in the 17th century. Duxelle can be made from wild or cultivated mushrooms and refrigerated or frozen in ice cube portions for 10 days or 8 weeks respectively.

50 g / 2 oz / 4 tbsp unsalted butter

2 shallots, chopped

450 g / 1 lb wild and/or cultivated mushrooms, trimmed and finely chopped

1 sprig thyme, chopped

50 ml / 3 1/2 tbsp white wine or sherry

celery salt

freshly ground black pepper

1 Melt the butter in a large non-stick frying pan over a gentle heat, add the shallots and fry for 2–3 minutes to soften without browning.

2 *(Right)* Add the mushrooms, thyme and wine and simmer so that the mushroom juices run, then increase the heat to boil off moisture. When quite dry, season with celery salt and pepper, if using straight away. Otherwise, cool and refrigerate or freeze.

Mushroom Purée

Mushroom purée takes Duxelle a stage further and reduces it to a fine purée. Mushroom purée is used mainly for the enrichment of soups, and sauces, although a spoonful works wonders in a casserole of beef or game. As with the Duxelle, mushroom purée freezes conveniently in ice cube portions.

1 Prepare the Duxelle as shown in the previous recipe. Spoon into a food processor and blend until smooth.

2 Allow to cool, transfer into an airtight jar and refrigerate for up to 10 days or freeze for up to 8 weeks.

Mushroom Extract

The finest edible mushrooms are best preserved whole or sliced. More common although less elegant species such as the field, horse and parasol mushroom lend their flavour and colour to a dark extract. It is very important to ensure mushrooms are properly identified before using. An incorrectly identified mushroom put among the others can cause fatal illness. Shaggy ink caps are worth putting in, as are any overgrown boletus mushrooms providing they are free from infestation and are in good condition. Any deterioration can cause the extract to ferment at a later date. The flavour extracted from the mushrooms will keep in the refrigerater in a screw-top jar or bottle for 8–10 weeks. Use readily to enliven and enrich winter soups, stews and game dishes.

450 g / 1 lb field, horse and parasol mushrooms, shaggy ink caps, orange birch bolete, slippery jack and/or winter chanterelles, trimmed and roughly chopped

300 ml / ½ pint / 1¼ cups water

200 ml / 7 fl oz / ⅞ cup red wine

60 ml / 4 tbsp dark soy sauce

5 ml / 1 tsp salt

1 sprig thyme

1 Place all of the ingredients in a large stainless steel pan. Bring to the boil and simmer uncovered for 45 minutes.

2 Strain the mushrooms through a nylon sieve, pressing as much liquid as possible back into the pan. Return the extract to the boil and reduce until half its volume.

3 *(Left)* Sterilize a preserving jar or bottle by immersing in boiling water for a few minutes. Drain. Fill the jar or bottle with the mushroom liquid, cover and allow to cool. When cool, label and store in the refrigerator. Mushroom extract can be frozen and used in ice cube portions.

Pickled Mushrooms

The principle of pickling eliminates the chance of bacterial growth by immersing mushrooms in vinegar. Vinegar can be flavoured and diluted to lessen the sharp taste. In this recipe shiitake mushrooms take on an oriental flavour, although other firm mushrooms and spices can also be used. It is best to dress pickled mushrooms with olive oil when serving, to restore balance. Serve as an appetizer or buffet style lunch item.

250 ml / 8 fl oz / 1 cup white wine vinegar
150 ml / 1/4 pint / 2/3 cup water
5 ml / 1 tsp salt
1 red chilli
10 ml / 2 tsp coriander seeds
10 ml / 2 tsp szechuan pepper or anise-pepper
250 g / 9 oz shiitake mushrooms, halved if large

1 Bring the wine vinegar and water to a simmer in a stainless steel pan. Add the salt, chilli, coriander, szechuan pepper or anise-pepper and mushrooms and cook for 10 minutes.

2 Sterilize a 500 ml / 18 fl oz / 2¼ cup preserving jar by immersing in boiling water. Drain until dry.

Transfer mushrooms and liquid to the jar, seal, label and leave for at least 10 days before trying.

Chanterelle Vodka

If you manage to find a few chanterelles on your mushroom foray, consider steeping them in vodka. Vodka has a neutral flavour and allows the apricot quality of the chanterelles to shine. Chill thoroughly before serving as an aperitif.

375 ml / 13 fl oz / 1½ cups vodka
75 g / 3 oz young chanterelle mushrooms, trimmed

1 Place the chanterelle mushrooms in a clean preserving bottle or jar.

2 Pour in the vodka, cover and leave at room temperature. Chanterelle vodka is ready when the mushrooms have dropped to the bottom.

Preserving Mushrooms in Oil

The method of preserving in oil is ideally suited to good quality firm mushrooms. The process can seem expensive, but the oil used takes on a delicious mushroom flavour which can then be used to make special salad dressings.

250 ml / 8 fl oz / 1 cup white wine vinegar

150 ml / ¼ pint / ⅔ cup water

5 ml / 1 tsp salt

1 sprig thyme

½ bay leaf

1 red chilli (optional)

450 g / 1 lb assorted wild mushrooms, including young bay boletus, chanterelles, saffron milk-caps and horn of plenty, trimmed and halved if large

400 ml / 14 fl oz / 1⅔ cups virgin olive oil

1 Bring the vinegar and water to a simmer in a stainless steel pan. Add the salt, thyme, bay leaf and chilli if using, and infuse for 15 minutes.

2 Add the mushrooms and simmer for 10 minutes. Sterilize a 500 ml / 18 fl oz / 2¼ cup preserving jar in boiling water. Drain until dry. Lift the cooked mushrooms out of the liquid, drain well and place in the jar.

3 (*Right*) Cover the mushrooms with oil, close the lid and label. Mushrooms in oil will keep in a cool place for up to 12 months.

Spiced Mushrooms in Alcohol

Winter chanterelles and oyster mushrooms combine with caraway seeds, lemon and chilli to make this unusual and warming infusion.

75 g / 3 oz winter chanterelle and oyster mushrooms

5 ml / 1 tsp caraway seeds

1 lemon

1 red chilli

375 ml / 13 fl oz / 1½ cups vodka

1 Place the mushrooms, caraway seeds, lemon and chilli in a clean preserving jar or bottle.

2 Pour in the vodka and leave for 2–3 weeks until the mushrooms no longer float. Chill thoroughly and serve as an aperitif.

Soups, Starters & Salads

Buckwheat Blinis with Mushroom Caviar

These little Russian pancakes are traditionally served with fish roe caviar and soured cream. The term caviar is also given to fine vegetable mixtures called ikry. This wild mushroom ikry caviar is popular in the autumn and has a silky rich texture.

SERVES 4

115 g / 4 oz / 1 cup strong white bread flour

50 g / 2 oz / 1/3 cup buckwheat flour

2.5 ml / 1/2 tsp salt

300 ml / 1/2 pint / 1 1/4 cups milk

5 ml / 1 tsp dried yeast

2 eggs, separated

For the Caviar

350 g / 12 oz mixed assorted wild mushrooms such as field mushrooms, orange birch bolete, bay boletus, oyster and St George's mushrooms

5 ml / 1 tsp celery salt

30 ml / 2 tbsp walnut oil

15 ml / 1 tbsp lemon juice

45 ml / 3 tbsp chopped fresh parsley

freshly ground black pepper

200 ml / 7 fl oz / scant 1 cup soured cream or crème fraîche

1 To make the caviar, trim and chop the mushrooms, then place them in a glass bowl, toss with the celery salt and cover with a weighted plate.

2 Leave the mushrooms for 2 hours until the juices have run out into the bottom of the bowl. Rinse the mushrooms thoroughly to remove the salt, drain and press out as much liquid as you can with the back of a spoon. Return them to the bowl and toss with walnut oil, lemon juice, parsley and a twist of pepper. Chill until ready to serve.

3 Sift the two flours together with the salt in a large mixing bowl. Warm the milk to approximately blood temperature. Add the yeast, stirring until dissolved, then pour into the flour, add the egg yolks and stir to make a smooth batter. Cover with a damp cloth and leave in a warm place.

4 Whisk the egg whites in a clean bowl until stiff then fold into the risen batter.

5 Heat an iron pan or griddle to a moderate temperature. Moisten with oil, then drop spoonfuls of the batter onto the surface. When bubbles rise to the surface, turn them over and cook briefly on the other side. Spoon on the soured cream, top with the mushroom caviar and serve.

Wild Mushroom Tapenade Toasts

Tapenade is a paste made from black olives, garlic, anchovies, capers, olive oil and lemon. A little goes a long way. Here it is spread on bread, toasted and topped with wild mushrooms and hard boiled eggs.

SERVES 4

350 g / 12 oz strongly flavoured wild mushrooms such as ceps, bay boletus, chicken of the woods, saffron milk-caps and chanterelles, trimmed and sliced

50 g / 2 oz / 4 tbsp unsalted butter

½ lemon

salt and freshly ground black pepper

4 small eggs

1 narrow French loaf, sliced

1 small bunch parsley, to garnish

For the Tapenade

150 g / 5 oz / 1 cup Kalamata olives, stoned

1 garlic clove, peeled

5 anchovy fillets

15 ml / 1 tbsp capers

30 ml / 2 tbsp olive oil

juice of ½ lemon

1 Fry the mushrooms gently in butter for 6–8 minutes to soften, then increase heat to evaporate the juices. Add a generous squeeze of lemon and season to taste. Transfer to a bowl, cover and keep warm.

2 To make the tapenade, place all the tapenade ingredients in a food processor and blend to a fine paste. Boil the eggs for 10 minutes.

3 Preheat a grill to a moderate temperature. Meanwhile cool the eggs under running cold water, peel and cut into quarters. Then slice the French loaf diagonally and toast on one side. Spread the other side thinly with tapenade and toast again.

4 Heap each piece of toast with wild mushrooms, top with a section of hard boiled egg and garnish with a sprig of parsley.

Cook's Tip

If you don't have time to make your own tapenade, buy it ready prepared from delicatessens and specialist food stores.

French Onion and Morel Soup

French onion soup is appreciated for its light beefy taste. Few improvements can be made to this classic soup, but a few richly scented morel mushrooms will impart a worthwhile flavour.

SERVES 4

50 g / 2 oz / 4 tbsp unsalted butter, plus extra for spreading
15 ml / 1 tbsp vegetable oil
3 medium onions, sliced
900 ml / 1½ pints / 3¾ cups beef stock
75 ml / 5 tbsp Madeira or sherry
8 medium dried morel mushrooms
4 slices French bread
75 g / 3 oz / 1 cup Gruyère, Beaufort or Fontina cheese, grated
30 ml / 2 tbsp chopped fresh parsley

1 Melt the butter and oil in a large frying pan, add the onions and cook for 10–15 minutes until the onions are a rich mahogany brown colour.

Cook's Tip
The flavour and richness of this soup will improve with keeping. Refrigerate for up to 5 days.

2 Transfer the browned onions to a large saucepan, cover with beef stock, add the Madeira and the morels, then simmer for 20 minutes.

3 Preheat the grill to a moderate temperature and toast the French bread on both sides. Spread one side with butter and heap with grated cheese. Ladle the soup into four flameproof bowls, float the cheesy toasts on top and grill until crisp and brown. Alternatively, grill the cheese-topped toast, place one slice in each warmed soup bowl and ladle the hot soup over. The toast will float to the surface. Scatter with chopped parsley and serve.

Cep Soup with Parsley Sippets

The lasting aroma of the cep mushroom is caught in this delicious soup.

SERVES 4

50 g / 2 oz / 4 tbsp unsalted butter
2 medium onions, finely chopped
1 garlic clove
225 g / 8 oz fresh ceps or bay bolete, sliced, or 25 g / 1 oz / ½ cup dried
75 ml / 5 tbsp dry white wine
900 ml / 1½ pints / 3¾ cups boiling chicken stock
115 g / 4 oz floury potatoes, peeled and diced
1 sprig thyme
15 ml / 1 tbsp lemon juice
salt and freshly ground black pepper

For the Sippets

3 slices day-old bread
50 g / 2 oz / 4 tbsp butter
45 ml / 3 tbsp finely chopped fresh parsley

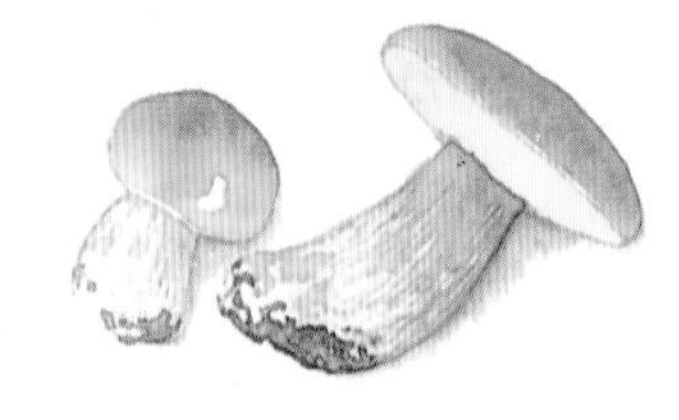

Cook's Tip
A variation on this soup can be made with the same quantity of dried saffron milk-caps or half the quantity of dried morel mushrooms.

1 Melt the butter in a large saucepan, add the onions and brown lightly. Add the garlic, ceps and wine. Add the stock, potatoes and thyme. Simmer gently for 45 minutes.

2 Liquidize the soup in just a few short bursts so that pieces of mushroom are left intact. Sharpen with lemon juice and season to taste.

3 To make the sippets, cut the bread into 2.5 cm / 1 in fingers. Melt the butter in a large frying pan, toss in the fingers of bread and fry until golden. Add the parsley and combine. Ladle the soup into warmed soup bowls, strew with parsley sippets and serve.

Tortellini Chanterelle Broth

The savoury-sweet quality of chanterelle mushrooms combines well in a simple broth with spinach-and-ricotta-filled tortellini. Serve as a starter or light main course.

SERVES 4

350 g / 12 oz fresh spinach and ricotta tortellini, or 175 g / 6 oz dried

1.2 litres / 2 pints / 5 cups chicken stock

75 ml / 5 tbsp dry sherry

175 g / 6 oz fresh chanterelle mushrooms, trimmed and sliced, or 15 g / ½ oz / ¼ cup dried

chopped fresh parsley, to garnish

1 Cook the tortellini according to the packet instructions.

2 Bring the chicken stock to the boil, add the sherry and mushrooms and simmer for 10 minutes.

3 Strain the tortellini, add to the stock, ladle into four warmed soup bowls and garnish with the chopped parsley.

Cook's Tip

For a lighter version, replace the tortellini with 115 g / 4 oz / 2 cups dried vermicelli pasta.

Champignons de Paris à la Grècque

Cultivated mushrooms are often criticized by serious mushroom pickers for a lack of flavour, but the *champignon de Paris* or chestnut mushroom is an improvement on the ubiquitous button mushroom.

SERVES 4

45 ml / 3 tbsp olive oil

15 button onions, peeled

½ garlic clove, crushed

675 g / 1½ lb Paris mushrooms or closed field mushrooms, halved or quartered if large

300 ml / ½ pint / 1¼ cups chicken stock, boiling

75 ml / 5 tbsp white wine

10 ml / 2 tsp black peppercorns

20 ml / 4 tsp coriander seeds

1 sprig thyme

1 small bay leaf

salt and freshly ground black pepper, if necessary

15 ml / 1 tbsp wine vinegar

15 cherry tomatoes

1 Heat the olive oil in a large non-stick frying pan. Add the onions and brown gently over a low heat. Add the garlic and the mushrooms, stir and fry gently until the mushrooms soften and the juices begin to run. Transfer to a large saucepan.

Cook's Tip

The flavour of these mushrooms will improve if kept refrigerated for up to a week. To peel button onions, cover with boiling water to soften their skins.

2 Add the stock, wine, peppercorns, coriander seeds, thyme and bay leaf. Cover the surface with a round of greaseproof paper. Simmer for 15 minutes. Add the vinegar and season if required.

3 Cover the cherry tomatoes with boiling water to loosen their skins, peel and add to the onion and mushroom mixture. Allow to cool to room temperature and serve with a basket of open textured bread.

Salad of Fresh Ceps with a Parsley, Egg and Walnut Dressing

To capture the just picked flavour of a cep or bay boletus, consider this delicious salad enriched with an egg yolk and walnut oil dressing. Choose small ceps and bay boletus for a firm texture and a fine flavour.

SERVES 4

350 g / 12 oz fresh ceps or bay boletus

175 g / 6 oz mixed salad leaves, to include: bativia, young spinach and frisée

salt and freshly ground black pepper

50 g / 2 oz / ½ cup broken walnut pieces, toasted

50 g / 2 oz fresh Parmesan cheese

For the Dressing

2 egg yolks

2.5 ml / ½ tsp French mustard

75 ml / 5 tbsp groundnut oil

45 ml / 3 tbsp walnut oil

30 ml / 2 tbsp lemon juice

30 ml / 2 tbsp chopped fresh parsley

1 pinch caster sugar

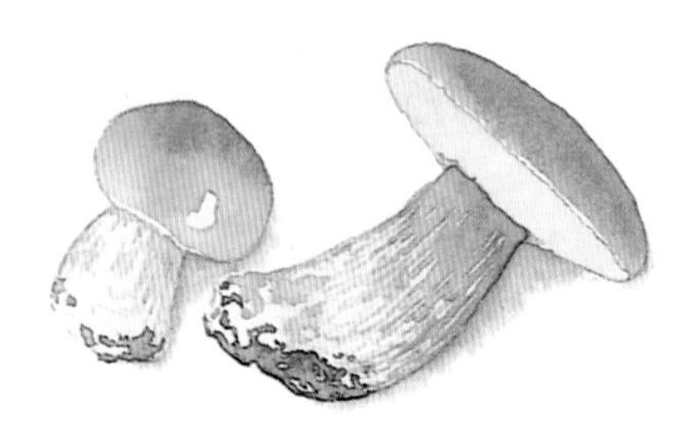

1 Place the egg yolks in a screw top jar with the mustard, groundnut and walnut oil, lemon juice, parsley and sugar. Shake well.

2 Slice the mushrooms thinly.

3 Place the mushrooms in a large salad bowl and combine with the dressing. Leave for 10–15 minutes for the flavours to mingle.

4 Wash and spin the salad leaves, then toss with the mushrooms.

5 Turn out onto four large plates, season well then scatter with toasted walnuts and shavings of Parmesan cheese.

Cook's Tip

For special occasions, 2–3 drops of truffle oil will impart a deep and mysterious flavour of the forests.

Cook's Tip

The dressing for this salad uses raw egg yolks. Be sure to use only the freshest eggs from a reputable supplier. Expectant mothers, young children and the elderly are not advised to eat raw egg yolks. If this presents a problem the dressing can be made without the egg yolks.

Shaggy Ink Cap and Parasol Mushroom Soup

The shaggy ink cap forms the basis of this creamy soup and the parasol mushrooms provide additional flavour.

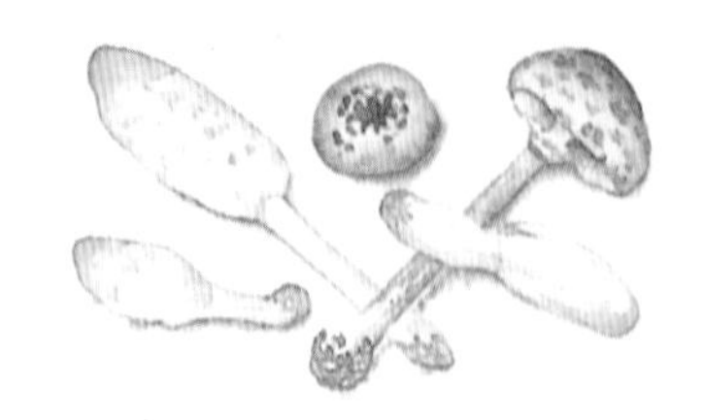

SERVES 4

50 g / 2 oz / 4 tbsp unsalted butter

4 shallots or 1 medium onion, chopped

225 g / 8 oz shaggy ink caps, closed specimens, trimmed and chopped

1 garlic clove, crushed

900 ml / 1½ pints / 3¾ cups chicken stock, boiling

175 g / 6 oz parasol mushrooms, caps and young stems, trimmed and sliced

60 ml / 4 tbsp double cream

30 ml / 2 tbsp lemon juice

salt and freshly ground black pepper

45 ml / 3 tbsp chopped fresh parsley

1 Melt half of the butter in a saucepan, add the shallots or onion and soften over a gentle heat.

2 Add the ink caps and garlic, and fry gently until the mushrooms soften and the juices begin to run.

3 Add the chicken stock, bring back to the boil and simmer for 15 minutes. Liquidize and return to the saucepan.

4 Melt the remaining butter in a non-stick frying pan, add the parasol mushrooms and fry to soften without letting them colour. Add to the saucepan and simmer for a minute.

5 Stir in the cream, sharpen with lemon juice, then season to taste. Ladle into four warmed soup bowls, scatter with parsley and serve with broken bread.

Cook's Tip

For best results, use closed ink caps that haven't started to blacken. Once they have begun to blacken they are quite safe to eat, but they will darken the colour of the soup.

An Artichoke Lover's Feast

Artichokes are a rich earthy vegetable which make a wonderful starter stuffed to the brim with a variety of cultivated and woodland mushrooms.

SERVES 4

4 large globe artichokes

1 lemon, sliced

25 g / 1 oz / 2 tbsp butter

2 shallots or 1 small onion, chopped

225 g / 8 oz assorted wild and cultivated mushrooms such as ceps, bay boletus, chanterelles, saffron milk-caps, oyster mushrooms, St George's, Caesar's and closed field mushrooms, trimmed and chopped

15 ml / 1 tbsp chopped fresh thyme

For the Hollandaise Sauce

175 g / 6 oz / ¾ cup unsalted butter

2 egg yolks

juice of ½ lemon

salt and freshly ground black pepper

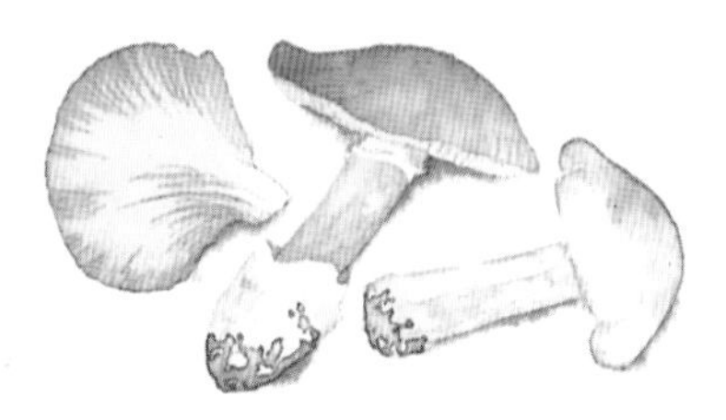

1 Bring a large saucepan of salted water to the boil. With a serrated knife remove one third from the top of each artichoke. Pull off the outer leaves and discard. Break off the artichoke stems at the base, then trim about 5 mm / ¼ in from the base. To prevent the artichokes from darkening tie a slice of lemon to the base. Place in the boiling water and cook for 25 minutes.

2 To make the mushroom filling, fry the shallots gently in butter to soften without letting them colour. Add the mushrooms and thyme, cover and cook until the juices begin to run. Increase the heat and allow the juices to evaporate. Keep warm.

3 When the artichokes are cooked (a small knife inserted in the base will indicate whether it is tender) drain and cool under running water. Remove the lemon slices and drain the artichokes upside down. To create a central cavity, pull out the small leaves from the middle of each artichoke then scrape out the fibrous choke.

4 To make the sauce, melt the butter skimming off any surface scum. Pour into a jug leaving behind the milky residue. Place the egg yolks in a glass bowl over a saucepan of 2.5cm / 1 in simmering water. Add 2.5 ml / ½ tsp water to the egg yolks and whisk until thick and foamy. Remove from the heat, then add the butter in a thin stream, whisking all the time. Add the lemon juice and a little boiling water to thin the sauce. Season to taste.

5 Combine one third of the sauce with the mushroom mixture and fill each of the artichokes. Serve at room temperature with the extra sauce.

Spinach with Wild Mushroom Soufflé

Wild mushrooms combine especially well with eggs and spinach in this sensational soufflé. Almost any combination of mushrooms can be used for this recipe although the firmer varieties provide the best texture.

SERVES 4

225 g / 8 oz fresh spinach, washed, or 115 g / 4 oz frozen chopped spinach

50 g / 2 oz / 4 tbsp unsalted butter, plus extra for greasing

1 garlic clove, crushed

175 g / 6 oz assorted wild mushrooms such as ceps, bay boletus, saffron milk-caps, oyster, field and Caesar's mushrooms

200 ml / 7 fl oz / 1 cup milk

45 ml / 3 tbsp plain flour

6 eggs, separated

salt and freshly ground black pepper

pinch grated nutmeg

25 g / 1 oz / ⅛ cup freshly grated Parmesan cheese

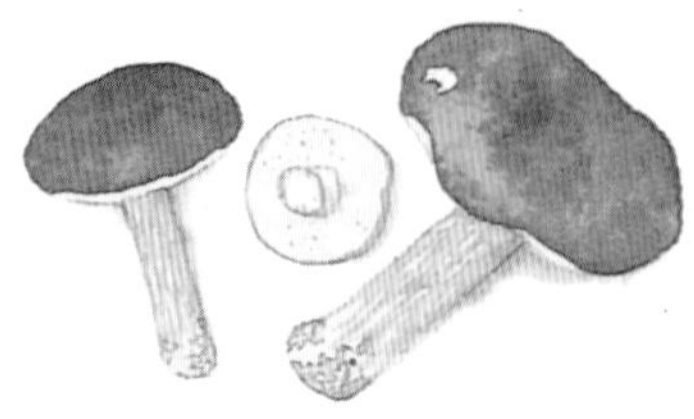

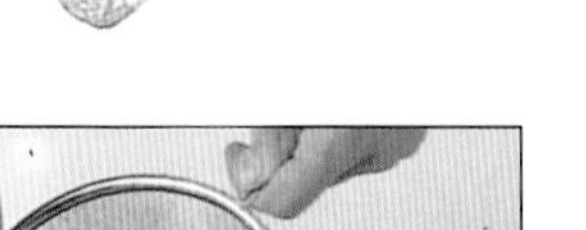

1 Preheat the oven to 190°C / 375°F / Gas 5. Steam the spinach over a moderate heat for 3–4 minutes. Cool under running water, then drain. Press out as much liquid as you can with the back of a large spoon and chop finely. If using frozen spinach, defrost and squeeze dry in the same way.

2 Gently soften the garlic and mushrooms in butter. Turn up the heat and evaporate the juices. When dry, add the spinach and transfer to a bowl. Cover and keep warm.

Cook's Tip
The soufflé base can be prepared up to 12 hours in advance and reheated before the beaten egg whites are folded in.

3 Measure 45 ml / 3 tbsp of the milk into a basin. Bring the remainder to the boil. Stir the flour and egg yolks into the milk in the basin and blend well. Stir the boiling milk into the egg and flour mixture, return to the pan and simmer to thicken. Add the spinach mixture. Season to taste with salt, pepper and nutmeg.

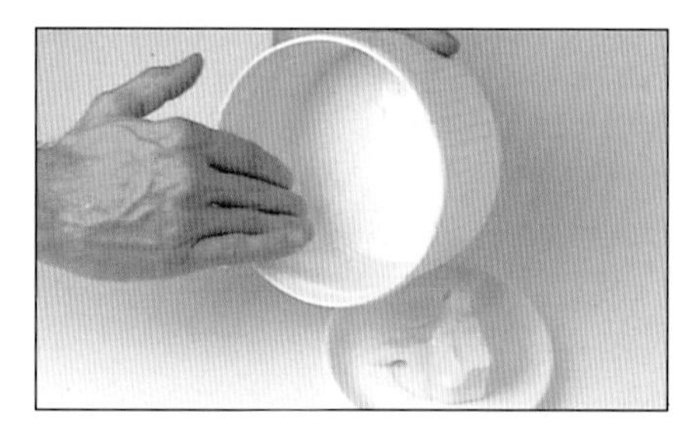

4 Butter a 900 ml / 1½ pint / 3¾ cups soufflé dish, paying particular attention to the sides. Sprinkle with a little of the cheese. Set aside.

5 Whisk the egg whites until they hold their weight on the whisk. Bring the spinach mixture back to the boil. Stir in a spoonful of beaten egg white, then fold the mixture into the remaining egg white. Turn into the soufflé dish, spread level, scatter with the remaining cheese and bake in the oven for about 25 minutes until well risen and golden.

Alsatian Tart

Alsace is renowned for its abundance of wild mushrooms. This tart is good with a cool Alsatian wine.

SERVES 4

350 g / 12 oz shortcrust pastry, thawed if frozen

50 g / 2 oz / 4 tbsp unsalted butter

3 medium onions, halved and sliced

350 g / 12 oz assorted wild mushrooms such as ceps, bay boletus, morels, chanterelles, saffron milk-caps, oyster, field and Caesar's mushrooms

leaves of 1 sprig thyme, chopped

salt and freshly ground black pepper

pinch of grated nutmeg

50 ml / 3½ tbsp full-fat milk

50 ml / 3½ tbsp single cream

1 egg and 2 egg yolks

1 Preheat the oven to 190°C / 375°F / Gas 5 and lightly grease a 23 cm / 9 in loose bottomed flan tin with butter. Roll out the pastry on a lightly floured board and line the tin. Rest the pastry in the fridge for 1 hour.

Cook's Tip
To prepare ahead, the flan case can be part baked and the filling made in advance. Continue from step 3.

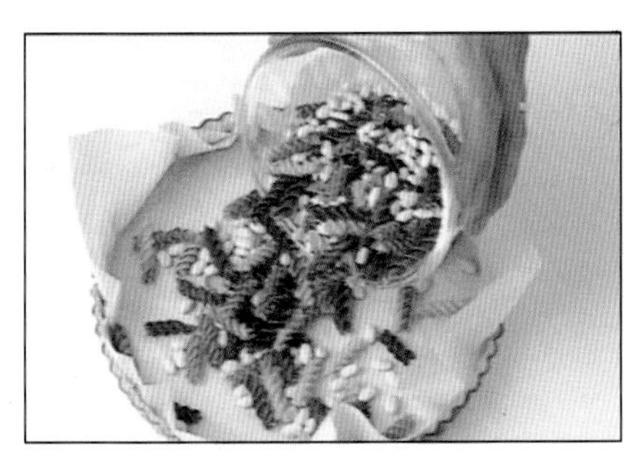

2 Place three squares of tissue paper in the flan case, fill with rice and bake blind for 25 minutes. Lift out the paper and rice and leave to cool.

3 Melt the butter in a frying pan, add the onions, cover and cook slowly for 20 minutes. Add the mushrooms and thyme, and continue cooking for a further 10 minutes. Season with salt, pepper and nutmeg.

4 Place the milk and cream in a jug and beat in the egg and egg yolks. Place the mushroom mixture in the flan case and then pour over the milk and egg mixture. Bake for 15–20 minutes until the centre is firm to the touch.

Stuffed Garlic Mushrooms with Prosciutto and Herbs

SERVES 4

1 medium onion, chopped
75 g / 3 oz / 6 tbsp unsalted butter
8 medium field mushrooms
15 g / ½ oz / ¼ cup dried ceps, bay boletus or saffron milk-caps, soaked in warm water for 20 minutes
1 garlic clove, crushed
75 g / 3 oz / ¾ cup fresh breadcrumbs
1 egg
75 ml / 5 tbsp chopped fresh parsley
15 ml / 1 tbsp chopped fresh thyme
salt and freshly ground black pepper
115 g / 4 oz prosciutto di Parma or San Daniele, thinly sliced
fresh parsley, to garnish

Cook's Tip
Garlic mushrooms can be easily prepared in advance ready to go into the oven.

1 Preheat the oven to 190°C / 375 °F / Gas 5. Fry the onion gently in half the butter for 6–8 minutes until soft but not coloured. Meanwhile, break off the stems of the field mushrooms, setting the caps aside. Drain the dried mushrooms and chop these and the stems of the field mushrooms finely. Add to the onion together with the garlic and cook for a further 2–3 minutes.

2 Transfer the mixture to a bowl, add the breadcrumbs, egg, herbs and seasoning. Melt the remaining butter in a small pan and generously brush over the mushroom caps. Arrange the mushrooms on a baking sheet and spoon in the filling. Bake in the oven for 20–25 minutes until well browned.

3 Top each with a strip of prosciutto, garnish with parsley and serve.

Mushroom Salad with Parma Ham

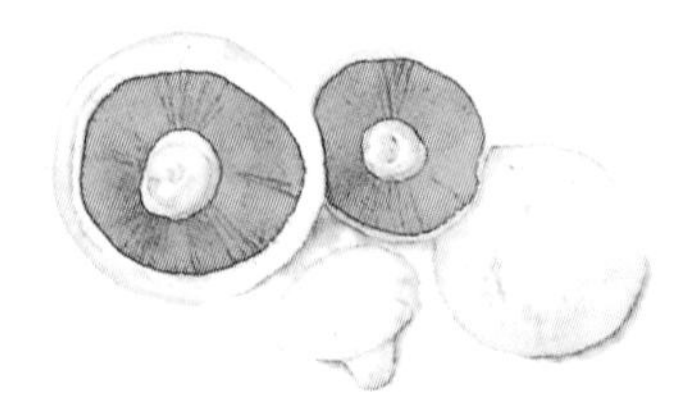

SERVES 4

40 g / 1½ oz / 3 tbsp unsalted butter
450 g / 1 lb assorted wild and cultivated mushrooms such as chanterelles, ceps, bay boletus, Caesar's mushrooms, oyster, field and Paris mushrooms, trimmed and sliced
60 ml / 4 tbsp Madeira or sherry
juice of ½ lemon
½ oak leaf lettuce
½ frisée lettuce
30 ml / 2 tbsp walnut oil

For the Pancake Ribbons

30 g / 1 oz / 3 tbsp plain flour
75 ml / 5 tbsp milk
1 egg
60 ml / 4 tbsp freshly grated Parmesan cheese
60 ml / 4 tbsp chopped fresh herbs such as parsley, thyme, marjoram or chives
salt and freshly ground black pepper
175 g / 6 oz Parma ham, thickly sliced

1 To make the pancakes, blend the flour and the milk. Beat in the egg, cheese, herbs and seasoning. Pour enough of the mixture into a frying pan to coat the bottom of it. When the batter has set, turn the pancake over and cook briefly on the other side.

2 Turn out and cool. Roll up the pancake and slice thinly to make 1 cm / ½ in ribbons. Cook the remaining batter in the same way and cut the ham into similar sized ribbons. Toss with the pancake ribbons.

3 Gently soften the mushrooms in the remaining butter for 6–8 minutes until the moisture has evaporated. Add the Madeira and lemon juice, and season to taste.

4 Toss the salad leaves in the oil and arrange on four plates. Place the ham and pancake ribbons in the centre, spoon on the mushrooms and serve.

Woodland Salsa Dip

This recipe makes good use of mushrooms that soften when cooked. Firmer-fleshed mushrooms can be added to provide texture and flavour.

SERVES 4

75 ml / 5 tbsp olive oil
1 medium onion, chopped
1 garlic clove, crushed
450 g / 1 lb aubergines, chopped
350 g / 12 oz shaggy ink caps, orange birch bolete and slippery jacks, trimmed and chopped
75 g / 3 oz chanterelles, charcoal burner or saffron milk caps, trimmed and chopped
45 ml / 3 tbsp chopped fresh parsley, chervil and chives
15 ml / 1 tbsp balsalmic vinegar
salt and freshly ground black pepper

For Dipping

sesame bread sticks, celery, carrot, baby sweetcorn, strips of toasted pitta bread

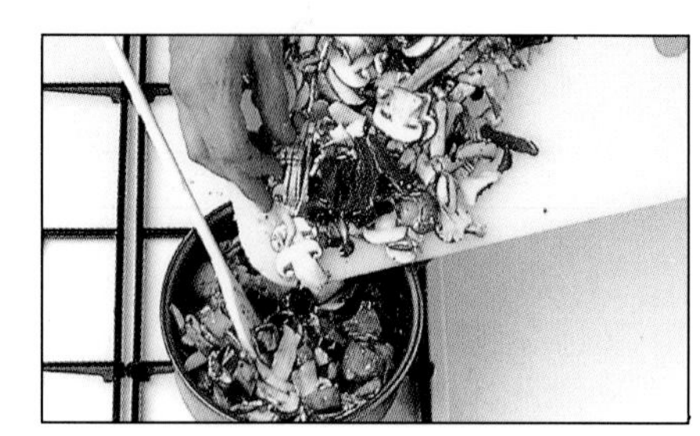

1 Heat 15 ml / 1 tbsp of the olive oil in a heavy saucepan over a moderate heat, add the onion and cook gently to soften without colouring.

2 Stir in the remaining oil, the garlic and aubergines, then cover and cook for 10 minutes. Add the mushrooms and cook uncovered for a further 15 minutes.

3 Stir in the herbs and vinegar and season to taste. Allow to cool and serve with bread sticks, pitta bread and raw vegetables.

Cook's Tip
Woodland salsa dip will keep in the fridge in a covered container for 10 days. Do not freeze it.

Spinach and Wild Mushroom Soup

SERVES 4

25 g / 1 oz / 2 tbsp unsalted butter
1 medium onion, chopped
350 g / 12 oz assorted wild and cultivated mushrooms such as ceps, bay boletus, orange birch bolete, shaggy ink caps, field, oyster and shiitake mushrooms, trimmed and chopped
1 garlic clove, crushed
10 ml / 2 tsp chopped fresh thyme or 5 ml / 1 tsp dried
1.2 litres / 2 pints / 5 cups boiling chicken or vegetable stock
75 g / 3 oz floury potato, finely chopped
400 g / 14 oz fresh spinach, trimmed, or 200 g / 7 oz frozen chopped spinach, defrosted and drained
salt and freshly ground black pepper
pinch of grated nutmeg
60 ml / 4 tbsp double or soured cream, to serve

Cook's Tip
If fresh wild mushrooms are unavailable, use 225 g / 8 oz cultivated field mushrooms with 10 g / ½ oz / ¼ cup dried ceps, bay boletus or saffron milk-caps.

1 Melt the butter in a large pan, add the onion and fry gently without colouring for 6–8 minutes. Add the mushrooms, garlic and herbs, cover and allow the moisture to run.

2 Add half of the stock, the potato and spinach. Bring back to the boil and simmer for 10 minutes.

3 Liquidize the soup and return to the saucepan. Add the remaining stock and season to taste with salt, pepper and a little nutmeg. Serve with a dollop of cream stirred into the soup.

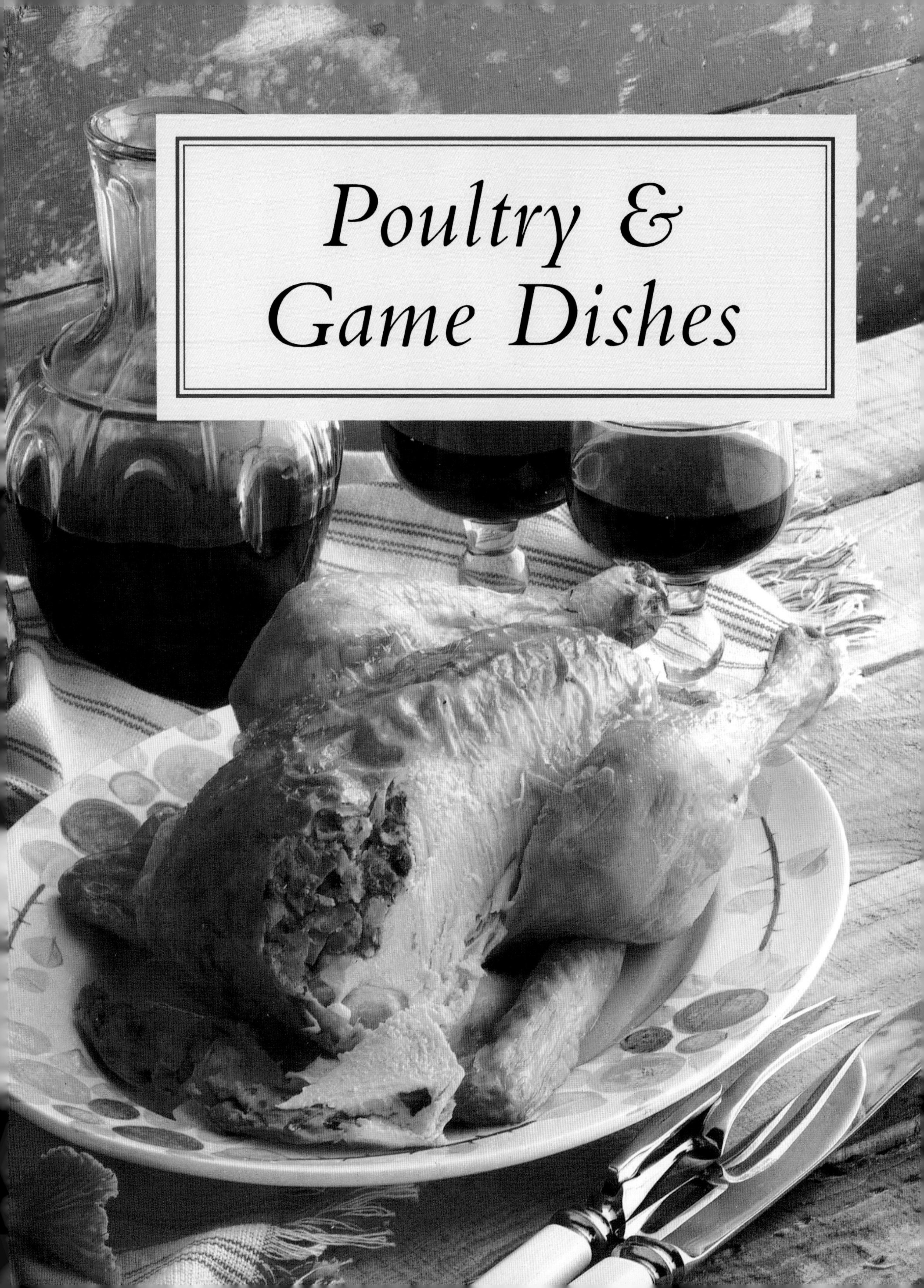
Poultry &
Game Dishes

Mushroom Picker's Chicken Paella

A good paella is based on a few well chosen ingredients. Here, wild mushrooms combine with chicken and vegetables.

SERVES 4

45 ml / 3 tbsp olive oil

1 medium onion, chopped

1 small bulb fennel, sliced

225 g / 8 oz assorted wild and cultivated mushrooms such as ceps, bay boletus, chanterelles, saffron milk-caps, hedgehog fungus, St George's, Caesar's and oyster mushrooms, trimmed and sliced

1 garlic clove, crushed

3 free range chicken legs, chopped through the bone

350 g / 12 oz / 1⅔ cups short-grain Spanish or Italian rice

900 ml / 1½ pints / 3¾ cups chicken stock, boiling

1 pinch saffron strands or 1 sachet of saffron powder

1 sprig thyme

400 g / 14 oz can butter beans, drained

75 g / 3 oz / ¾ cup frozen peas

1 Heat the olive oil in a 35 cm / 14 in paella pan or a large frying pan. Add the onion and fennel and fry over a gentle heat for 3–4 minutes.

2 Add the mushrooms and garlic, and cook until the juices begin to run, then increase the heat to evaporate the juices. Push the onion and mushrooms to one side. Add the chicken pieces and fry briefly.

3 Stir in the rice, add the stock, saffron, thyme, butter beans and peas. Bring to a simmer and then cook gently for 15 minutes without stirring.

4 Remove from the heat and cover the surface of the paella with a circle of greased greaseproof paper. Cover the paper with a clean tea towel and allow the paella to finish cooking in its own heat for about 5 minutes. Bring to the table, uncover and serve.

Cook's Tip

For a vegetarian mushroom paella, omit the chicken, replace the chicken stock with vegetable stock and if you can, include chicken of the woods in your choice of mushrooms.

"Chicken" of the Woods Polenta with a Cauliflower Fungus Cream

This dish contains no chicken at all and will please both meat eaters and vegetarians alike. So convincing is the flavour and texture of chicken of the woods, that many people will find it difficult to believe that they're not actually eating chicken.

SERVES 4

450 g / 1 lb small new potatoes

1.3 litres / 2¼ pints / 5½ cups light vegetable stock, boiling

175 g / 6 oz young carrots, trimmed and peeled

175 g / 6 oz sugar snap peas

50 g / 2 oz / 4 tbsp unsalted butter

75 g / 3 oz Caesar's mushrooms or hedgehog fungus, trimmed and sliced

5 horn of plenty, fresh or dried, chopped

250 g / 9 oz / 1½ cups fine polenta or cornmeal

2 shallots or 1 small onion, chopped

2 fist-sized pieces cauliflower fungus or 15 g / ½ oz / ¼ cup dried

115 g / 4 oz chicken of the woods, trimmed and sliced

150 ml / ¼ pint / ⅔ cup single cream

3 egg yolks

10 ml / 2 tsp lemon juice

celery salt and cayenne pepper

Cook's Tip

If preparing this recipe in advance, make the polenta loaf and mushroom and vegetable sauce then allow to cool. When ready to serve, reheat the polenta and sauce, then thicken the sauce with egg yolks, season and serve.

1 Lightly oil a 23 cm / 9 in loaf tin and line with a single sheet of greaseproof paper. Set aside. Cover the potatoes with boiling water, add a pinch of salt and cook for 20 minutes. Bring the vegetable stock to the boil, add the carrots and peas and cook for 3–4 minutes. Remove with a slotted spoon and keep warm.

2 Add 25 g / 1 oz / 2 tbsp of the butter and the Caesar's mushrooms or hedgehog fungus and horn of plenty to the stock and simmer for 5 minutes. Introduce the polenta in a steady stream and stir for 2–3 minutes until thickened. Turn the polenta into the prepared tin, cover and allow to become firm.

3 To make the sauce, melt the remaining butter, add the shallots or onion and cook gently without colouring. Add the cauliflower fungus cut into thumb-sized pieces, with the chicken of the woods, and cook for 2–3 minutes. Add the cream and the reserved cooked vegetables and simmer to eliminate excess moisture.

4 Remove from the heat, stir in the egg yolks and allow residual heat to slightly thicken the sauce. The sauce must not boil at this stage. Add the lemon juice, then season with celery salt and a dash of cayenne pepper.

5 To serve, turn the warm polenta out onto a board, slice with a wet knife and arrange on four serving plates. Spoon the mushroom and vegetable sauce over the polenta.

St George's Chicken Cobbler

The St George's mushroom, so named because it emerges near to St George's day, 23rd April, combines especially well with chicken in this traditional English cobbler. If St George's mushrooms are not available, use a mixture of bay boletus, saffron milk-caps, parasol mushroom, yellow russula, oyster or closed field mushrooms.

SERVES 4

60 ml / 4 tbsp vegetable oil
1 medium onion, chopped
1 celery stick, sliced
1 small carrot, peeled and cut into julienne strips
3 chicken breasts, skin and bone removed
450 g / 1 lb St George's mushrooms or a selection of others mentioned above, trimmed and sliced
75 g / 3 oz / 6 tbsp plain flour
500 ml / 18 fl oz / 2¼ cups chicken stock, boiling
10 ml / 2 tsp Dijon mustard
30 ml / 2 tbsp medium sherry
10 ml / 2 tsp wine vinegar
salt and freshly ground black pepper

For the Cobbler Topping

275 g / 10 oz / 2½ cups self-raising flour
pinch of celery salt
pinch of cayenne pepper
115 g / 4 oz / ½ cup firm unsalted butter, diced
50 g / 2 oz / ½ cup Cheddar cheese, grated
150 ml / ¼ pint / ⅔ cup cold water
1 beaten egg, to glaze, optional

1 Preheat the oven to 200°C / 400°F / Gas 6. Heat the oil in a large heavy saucepan, add the onion, celery and carrot and fry gently without colouring, to soften. Cut the chicken breasts into bite-sized pieces, add to the vegetables and cook briefly. Add the mushrooms, fry until the juices run, then stir in the flour.

2 Remove the pan from the heat and stir in the stock gradually so that the flour is completely absorbed. Return the pan to the heat, and simmer gently to thicken, stirring all the time. Add the mustard, sherry, vinegar and seasoning. Cover and keep warm.

Cook's Tip

This recipe can easily be made as a pie by replacing the cobbler topping with a layer of flaky or shortcrust pastry.

3 To make the topping, sift the flour, celery salt and cayenne pepper into a bowl or a food processor fitted with a metal blade. Add the butter and half of the cheese, then either rub the mixture together with your fingers or process until it resembles large fresh breadcrumbs. Add the water and combine without over mixing.

4 Turn out onto a floured board, form into a round and flatten to about a 1.5 cm / ½ in thickness. Cut out as many 5 cm / 2 in shapes as you can, using a plain cutter.

5 Transfer the chicken mixture to a 1.2 litre / 2 pint / 5 cup pie dish, then overlap the cobbler shapes around the edge. Brush with beaten egg, scatter with the remaining cheese and bake in the oven for 25–30 minutes until the topping is well risen and golden.

Sherry Braised Guinea Fowl with Saffron Milk-caps

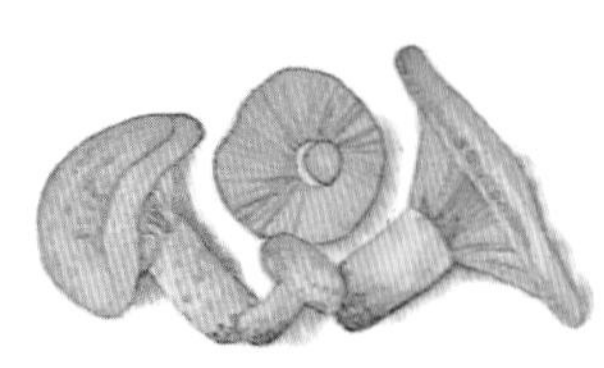

SERVES 4

2 young guinea fowl, tied
salt and freshly ground black pepper
50 g / 2 oz / 4 tbsp unsalted butter
75 ml / 5 tbsp dry sherry
2 medium onions, sliced
1 small carrot, peeled and chopped
½ celery stick, chopped
225 g / 8 oz assorted wild mushrooms such as saffron milk-caps or chanterelles, oyster, St George's, parasol and field mushrooms, trimmed and sliced
450 ml / ¾ pint / 1⅞ cup chicken stock, boiling
1 sprig thyme
1 bay leaf
15 ml / 1 tbsp lemon juice

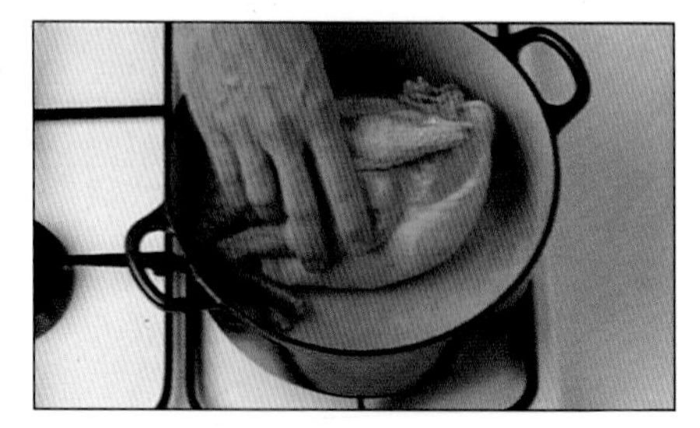

1 Preheat the oven to 190°C / 375°F / Gas 5. Season the guinea fowl with salt and pepper. Melt half of the butter in a flameproof casserole, add the birds and turn until browned all over. Transfer to a shallow dish, heat the sediment in the pan, pour in the sherry and bring to the boil, stirring to deglaze the pan. Pour this liquid over the birds and set aside.

Cook's Tip

If fresh wild mushrooms are unavailable substitute with 15 g / ½ oz / ¼ cup of dried saffron milk-caps or ceps, with 75 g / 3 oz cultivated oyster or field mushrooms.

2 Wipe the casserole clean, then melt the remaining butter. Add the onions, carrots and celery. Place the birds on top, cover and cook in the oven for 40 minutes.

3 Add the chicken stock and the thyme and bay leaf. Tie the mushrooms into a 30 cm / 12 in square of muslin. Place in the casserole, cover and return to the oven for a further 40 minutes.

4 Transfer the birds to a serving platter, remove the thyme and bay leaf and set the mushrooms in the bag aside. Liquidize the braising liquid and pour back into the casserole. Add the mushrooms from the muslin to the sauce. Season with salt and pepper and add lemon juice to taste. Heat until simmering and serve over the guinea fowl or pour into a serving jug.

Braised Pheasant with Ceps, Chestnuts and Bacon

Pheasant at the end of their season are not suitable for roasting, so consider this delicious casserole enriched with wild mushrooms and chestnuts. Allow two birds for four people.

SERVES 4

2 mature pheasants

salt and freshly ground black pepper

50 g / 2 oz / 4 tbsp butter

75 ml / 5 tbsp brandy

12 button or pickling onions, peeled

1 celery stick, chopped

50 g / 2 oz unsmoked rindless bacon, cut into strips

45 ml / 3 tbsp plain flour

500 ml / 18 fl oz / 2¼ cups chicken stock, boiling

175 g / 6 oz peeled chestnuts

350 g / 12 oz fresh ceps or bay boletus, trimmed and sliced, or 15 g / ½ oz / ¼ cup dried, soaked in warm water for 20 minutes

15 ml / 1 tbsp lemon juice

watercress sprigs, to garnish

1 Preheat the oven to 170°C / 325°F / Gas 3. Season the pheasants with salt and pepper. Melt half of the butter in a large flameproof casserole and brown the pheasants over a moderate heat. Transfer to a shallow dish and pour off the cooking fat. Return the casserole to the heat and brown the sediment. Stand back and add the brandy, (the sudden flames will die down quickly). Stir to loosen the sediment with a flat wooden spoon and then pour the juices over the pheasant.

2 Wipe the casserole and melt the remaining butter. Lightly brown the onions, celery and bacon. Stir in the flour. Remove from the heat.

3 Stir in the stock gradually so that it is completely absorbed by the flour. Add the chestnuts, mushrooms, the pheasants and their juices. Bring back to a gentle simmer, then cover and cook in the oven for 1½ hours.

Cook's Tip

Cooking and peeling fresh chestnuts can be hard work, so look out for canned or vacuum packed varieties.

4 Transfer the pheasants and vegetables to a serving plate. Bring the sauce back to the boil, add the lemon juice and season to taste. Pour the sauce into a jug and garnish the birds.

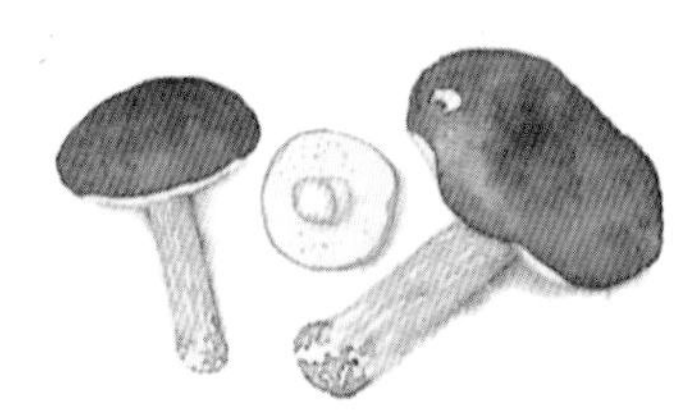

Chicken Fricassée Forestier

The term fricassée is used to describe a light stew, usually of chicken that is first sauteed in butter. The accompanying sauce can vary, but here wild mushrooms and bacon provide a rich woodland flavour.

SERVES 4

3 free range chicken breasts, sliced
salt and freshly ground black pepper
50 g / 2 oz / 4 tbsp unsalted butter
15 ml / 1 tbsp vegetable oil
115 g / 4 oz unsmoked rindless streaky bacon, cut into pieces
75 ml / 5 tbsp dry sherry or white wine
1 medium onion, chopped
350 g / 12 oz assorted wild mushrooms such as chanterelles, ceps, bay boletus, horn of plenty, chicken of the woods, hedgehog fungus, saffron milk-caps, closed field mushrooms and cauliflower fungus, trimmed and sliced
40 g / 1½ oz / 3 tbsp plain flour
500 ml / 18 fl oz / 2¼ cups chicken stock
10 ml / 2 tsp lemon juice
60 ml / 4 tbsp chopped fresh parsley

1 Season the chicken with pepper. Heat half of the butter and the oil in a large heavy skillet or flameproof casserole and brown the chicken and bacon pieces. Transfer to a shallow dish and pour off any excess fat.

Cook's Tip
It is worth spending a little extra on properly reared free range chicken. Not only is it less fatty, but it also has a better flavour and texture.

2 Return the skillet to the heat and brown the sediment. Pour in the sherry or wine and stir with a flat wooden spoon to deglaze the pan. Pour the sherry liquid over the chicken and wipe the skillet clean.

3 Fry the onion in the remaining butter until golden brown. Add the mushrooms and cook, stirring frequently, for 6–8 minutes, until their juices begin to run. Stir in the flour then remove from the heat. Gradually add the chicken stock and stir well until the flour is completely absorbed.

4 Add the reserved chicken and bacon with the sherry juices, return to the heat and stir to thicken. Simmer for 10–15 minutes and then add the lemon juice, parsley and seasoning. Serve with plain boiled rice, carrots and baby sweetcorn.

Pan Fried "Chicken" of the Woods with a Sherry Cream Sauce

This dish doesn't use real chicken, the flavour, texture and aroma of *Laetiporus sulphureus* or chicken of the woods is so similar to roast chicken, that it can be used in place of the real thing. There's no doubt that both vegetarians and meat eaters will enjoy this dish.

SERVES 4

50 g / 2 oz / 4 tbsp unsalted butter

2 shallots or 1 small onion, chopped

1 celery stick, sliced

½ medium carrot, peeled and sliced

350 g / 12 oz chicken of the woods, trimmed and sliced

50 g / 2 oz / 5 tbsp plain flour

450 ml / ¾ pint / 1⅞ cups chicken or vegetable stock

75 ml / 5 tbsp sherry

30 ml / 2 tbsp chopped fresh tarragon

75 ml / 5 tbsp double cream

30 ml / 2 tbsp lemon juice

celery salt and cayenne pepper

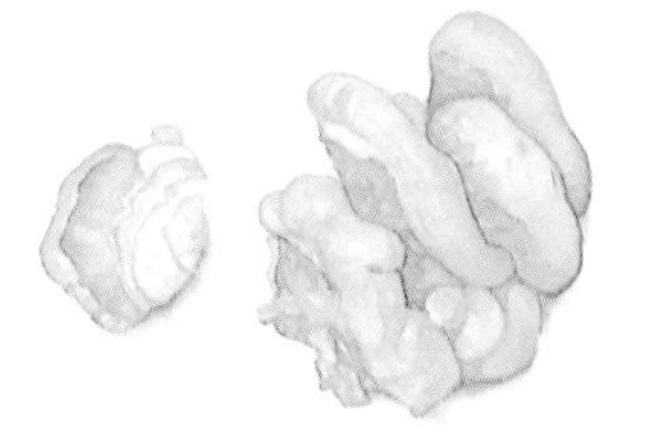

1 Melt the butter in a large skillet or flameproof casserole, add the shallots or onion, celery and carrot and fry gently until soft but without colouring.

2 Add the chicken of the woods, let them absorb some of the pan juices, then cook for 3–4 minutes. Stir in the flour and remove from the heat.

3 Gradually add the stock, stirring well so that the flour is absorbed. Heat gently until simmering, stirring all the time, then add the sherry and tarragon and simmer for 6–8 minutes.

4 Just before serving, stir in the cream and lemon juice and season to taste with celery salt and a dash of cayenne pepper. Serve over tagliatelle or fettuccine pasta.

Cook's Tip

Instead of serving it over pasta, try this recipe as a delicious pie filling. Cover with puff or shortcrust pastry and bake for 45–50 minutes at 190°C / 375°F / Gas 5.

Wild Duck Roasted with Morels and Madeira

Wild duck has a rich autumnal flavour that combines well with stronger-tasting mushrooms.

SERVES 4

- *2 × 1.1 kg / 2½ lb mallards, dressed and barded weight*
- *salt and freshly ground black pepper*
- *50 g / 2 oz / 4 tbsp unsalted butter*
- *75 ml / 5 tbsp Madeira or sherry*
- *1 medium onion, halved and sliced*
- *½ celery stick, chopped*
- *1 small carrot, chopped*
- *10 large dried morel mushrooms*
- *225 g / 8 oz blewits, parasol and field mushrooms, trimmed and sliced*
- *600 ml / 1 pint / 2½ cups chicken stock, boiling*
- *1 sprig thyme*
- *10 ml / 2 tsp wine vinegar*
- *parsley sprigs and carrot juliennes, to garnish*
- *game chips, to serve*

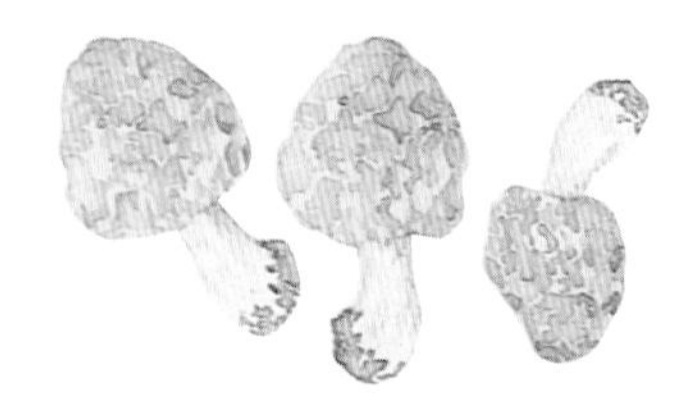

1 Preheat the oven to 190°C / 375°F / Gas 5 and season the ducks with salt and pepper. Melt half of the butter in a heavy skillet and brown the birds evenly. Transfer to a shallow dish, heat the sediment in the pan, pour in the Madeira or sherry and bring to the boil, stirring, to deglaze the pan. Pour this liquid over the birds and set aside.

2 Heat the remaining butter in a large flameproof casserole and add the onion, celery and carrot. Place the birds on top and cook in the oven for 40 minutes, reserving the juices.

3 Tie the mushrooms in a 46 cm / 18 in square piece of muslin. Add the stock, pan liquid, thyme and the muslin bag to the casserole. Cover and return to the oven for 40 minutes.

Cook's Tip

Mallard is the most popular wild duck, although widgeon and teal are good substitutes. A widgeon will serve two but allow one teal per person.

4 Transfer the birds to a serving platter, remove and discard the thyme and set the mushrooms aside. Liquidize the braising liquid and pour back into the casserole. Break open the muslin bag and stir the mushrooms into the sauce. Add the vinegar, season to taste and heat through gently. Garnish the ducks with parsley and carrot. Serve with game chips or crisps and the Madeira or sherry sauce.

Roast Chicken Stuffed with Forest Mushrooms

A good roast chicken is a feast of flavour and succulence. Spend a little more money on a free range bird and let its flavour mingle with the wild aroma of woodland mushrooms.

SERVES 4

25 g / 1 oz / 2 tbsp unsalted butter, plus extra for basting and to finish gravy

1 shallot, chopped

225 g / 8 oz wild mushrooms such as chanterelles, ceps, bay boletus, oyster, chicken of the woods, saffron milk-caps, and hedgehog fungus, trimmed and chopped

45 g / 1½ oz / ⅔ cup fresh white breadcrumbs

salt and freshly ground black pepper

2 egg yolks

1.75 kg / 4–4½ lb free range chicken

½ celery stick, chopped

½ small carrot, chopped

75 g / 3 oz potato, peeled and chopped

200 ml / 7 fl oz / 1 cup chicken stock, plus extra if required

10 ml / 2 tsp wine vinegar

parsley sprigs, to garnish

1 Preheat the oven to 220°C / 425°F / Gas 7. Melt the butter in a saucepan and gently fry the shallot without letting it colour. Add half of the chopped mushrooms and cook for 2–3 minutes until the moisture appears. Remove from the heat, stir in the breadcrumbs, seasoning and egg yolks, to bind.

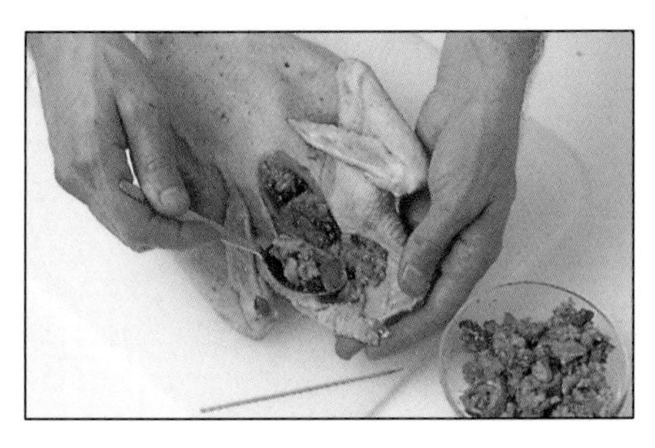

2 Spoon the stuffing into the neck of the chicken, enclose and fasten the skin on the underside with a skewer.

3 Rub the chicken with some extra butter and season well. Put the celery, carrot, potato and remaining mushrooms in the bottom of a roasting tin. Place the chicken on top of the vegetables, add the chicken stock and roast in the oven for 1¼ hours.

4 Transfer the chicken to a carving board or warmed serving plate, then liquidize the vegetables and mushrooms. Pour the mixture back into the tin and heat gently, adjusting the consistency with chicken stock if necessary. Taste and adjust seasoning then add the vinegar and a knob of butter and stir briskly. Pour the sauce into a serving jug and garnish the chicken with sprigs of parsley.

Cook's Tip

If fresh mushrooms are not available, replace with 15 g / ½ oz / ¼ cup of the dried equivalent and soak for 20 minutes before using.

Roast Turkey Flavoured with all Manner of Mushrooms

A roast turkey on the festive table tends to look better than it tastes. One sure way to boost its flavour and succulence is to stuff it with the season's wild mushrooms. The gravy too, can be flavoured with all manner of mushrooms.

SERVES 6–8

5 kg / 10 lb free range turkey, dressed weight

butter, for basting

watercress, to garnish

For the Mushroom Stuffing

50 g / 2 oz / 4 tbsp unsalted butter

1 medium onion, chopped

225 g / 8 oz wild mushrooms, such as chanterelle, ceps, bay boletus, chicken of the woods, saffron milk-caps, Caesar's mushrooms and hedgehog fungus, trimmed and chopped

75 g / 3 oz / 1½ cups fresh white breadcrumbs

115 g / 4 oz pork sausages, skinned

1 small fresh truffle, sliced (optional)

5 drops truffle oil (optional)

salt and freshly ground black pepper

For the Gravy

75 ml / 5 tbsp medium sherry

400 ml / 14 fl oz / 1⅔ cups chicken stock

15 g / ½ oz / ¼ cup dried ceps, soaked

20 ml / 4 tsp cornflour

5 ml / 1 tsp Dijon mustard

2.5 ml / ½ tsp wine vinegar

salt and freshly ground black pepper

1 Preheat the oven to 220°C / 425°F / Gas 7. To make the stuffing, melt the butter in a saucepan, add the onion and fry gently without colouring. Add the mushrooms and stir until their juices begin to flow. Remove from the heat, add the breadcrumbs, sausage meat and the truffle and truffle oil if using, season and stir well to combine.

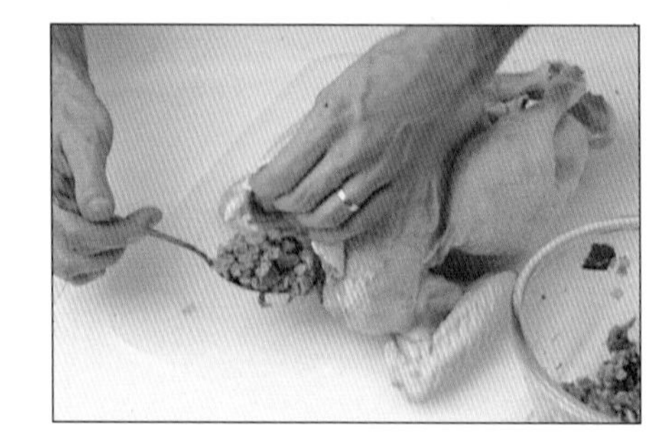

2 Spoon the stuffing into the neck cavity of the turkey and enclose, fastening the skin on the underside with a skewer.

3 Rub the skin of the turkey with butter, place in a large roasting tin uncovered and roast in the oven for 50 minutes. Lower the temperature to 180°C / 350°F / Gas 4 and cook for a further 2 hours and 30 minutes.

4 To make the gravy, transfer the turkey to a carving board, cover loosely with foil and keep warm. Spoon off the fat from the roasting tin and discard. Heat the remaining liquid until reduced to a sediment. Add the sherry and stir briskly with a flat wooden spoon to loosen the sediment. Stir in the chicken stock.

5 Place the cornflour and mustard in a cup, and blend with 10 ml / 2 tsp water and the wine vinegar. Stir this mixture into the juices in the basting tin and simmer to thicken. Season with salt and pepper and then stir in a knob of butter.

6 Garnish the turkey with bunches of watercress. Turn the gravy into a serving jug and serve separately.

Cook's Tip

Other sizes of turkey can be cooked this way – allow 675 g / 1½ lb dressed weight of turkey per person and roast for 20 minutes per 450 g / 1 lb.

Beef, Pork & Lamb

Sausage Popover with a Field Mushroom Gravy

The popover is made by pouring a simple batter over partly cooked sausages and baking in a fiercely hot oven. The intense heat is essential to its lightness and volume. To accompany this feast, a dark field mushroom gravy is served straight from the jug.

SERVES 4
675 g / 1½ lb pork sausages
15 ml / 1 tbsp vegetable oil
For the Batter
3 eggs
salt and freshly ground black pepper
115 g / 4 oz / 1 cup plain flour
300 ml / ½ pint / 1¼ cups full-fat milk
For the Mushroom Gravy
1 medium onion, chopped
25 g / 1 oz / 2 tbsp unsalted butter
175 g / 6 oz open cap field mushrooms, trimmed and sliced
1 sprig thyme, chopped
450 ml / ¾ pint / 1⅞ cups chicken stock, boiling
15 ml / 1 tbsp cornflour
15 ml / 1 tbsp mushroom ketchup or water
5 ml / 1 tsp Dijon mustard

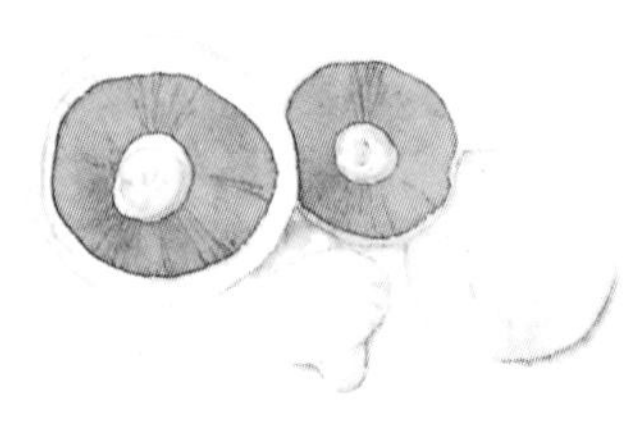

Cook's Tip
If you have time it is a good idea to leave the batter to rest for 30–40 minutes before using. This will ensure the finished popover has a lighter texture.

1 Preheat the oven to 230°C / 450°F / Gas 8. Prick the sausages and place them in a roasting tin with the oil. Cook in the oven for 10 minutes.

2 To make the batter, beat the eggs, season then add the flour and stir to make a smooth paste. Add the milk a little at a time. Pour over the sausages. Bake for 35–40 minutes, until the batter is well risen and crisp.

3 To make the gravy, lightly brown the onion in butter. Add the mushrooms and thyme and soften for 3–4 minutes until the juices begin to run. Add the stock and simmer.

4 Blend the cornflour with the ketchup or water and the mustard. Stir into the stock and simmer to thicken. Serve the popover with potatoes, broccoli, carrots and gravy.

Beef Goulash with Dark Mushrooms and Morels

A good Hungarian goulash is made rich and smooth with onions and paprika. In this recipe dark field mushrooms and morel mushrooms provide extra smoothness and a good depth of flavour.

SERVES 4

900 g / 2 lb chuck steak, diced

salt and freshly ground black pepper

60 ml / 4 tbsp vegetable oil

150 ml / ¼ pint / ⅔ cup red wine

4 medium onions, halved and sliced

450 g / 1 lb field or horse mushrooms or closed shaggy ink caps, trimmed and chopped

45 ml / 3 tbsp mild paprika

600 ml / 1 pint / 2½ cups beef stock

30 ml / 2 tbsp tomato purée

15 g / ½ oz / ¼ cup dried morel mushrooms, soaked in warm water for 20 minutes

15 ml / 1 tbsp wine vinegar

1 Preheat the oven to 170°C / 325°F / Gas 3 and season the meat with pepper. Heat half of the oil in a large frying pan and fry the meat over a high heat. A quantity of liquid will appear which must be evaporated before the meat will brown and take on flavour. When the meat has browned, transfer to a flameproof casserole and pour off the fat. Return the frying pan to the heat, add the wine and stir with a flat wooden spoon to deglaze the pan. Pour the liquid over the meat and wipe the pan clean.

2 Heat the remaining oil in the pan, add the onions and brown lightly.

3 Add the mushrooms, paprika, stock, tomato purée, the morels and their liquid to the casserole. Bring to a simmer, cover and cook in the oven for about 1½ hours.

Cook's Tip

Goulash can also be made with diced pork or veal. In this case use chicken stock in place of beef. To keep the goulash a good colour, select closed shaggy ink caps that have not started to blacken and deteriorate.

4 Just before serving, add the vinegar and adjust seasoning if necessary. Serve with jacket potatoes, Savoy cabbage and carrots.

Cep Meatballs with a Roquefort and Walnut Sauce

The salty rich acidity of Roquefort cheese enhances the flavour of good beef. In this recipe meatballs are flavoured with cep mushrooms. A Roquefort and walnut sauce makes it a dish to remember.

SERVES 4

15 g / ½ oz / ¼ cup dried ceps or bay boletus, soaked in warm water for 20 minutes

450 g / 1 lb lean minced beef

1 small onion, finely chopped

2 egg yolks

10 ml / 2 tsp chopped fresh thyme

celery salt and freshly ground black pepper

30 ml / 2 tbsp olive oil

For the Roquefort Sauce

200 ml / 7 fl oz / ⅞ cup milk

50 g / 2 oz walnuts, toasted

3 slices white bread, crusts removed

75 g / 3 oz Roquefort cheese

60 ml / 4 tbsp chopped fresh parsley

1 Drain the mushrooms, reserving the liquid, and chop finely. Place the beef, onion, egg yolks, thyme and seasoning in a bowl, add the mushrooms and combine well. Divide the mixture into thumb-sized pieces with wet hands and roll into balls.

2 To make the sauce, place the milk in a small pan and bring to a simmer. Put the walnuts in a food processor and grind smoothly, then add the bread and pour in the milk and reserved mushroom liquid. Add the cheese and parsley, then process smoothly. Transfer to a mixing bowl, cover and keep warm.

3 Heat the olive oil in a large non-stick frying pan. Cook the meatballs in two batches for 6–8 minutes. Add the sauce to the pan and heat very gently without allowing it to boil, then turn into a serving dish or serve over ribbon pasta.

Old English Steak and Mushroom Pudding

This pudding has been lost to the fast-food lifestyle. It takes five hours to cook but it is worth waiting for!

SERVES 4

450 g / 1 lb chuck steak, diced

225 g / 8 oz assorted wild and cultivated mushrooms such as chanterelles, ceps, orange birch bolete, shaggy ink caps, horn of plenty, saffron milk-caps, blewits, oyster, field and St George's mushrooms and not more than 3 dried morels, trimmed and sliced

1 medium onion, chopped

45 ml / 3 tbsp plain flour

celery salt and freshly ground black pepper

3 shakes Worcestershire sauce

120 ml / 4 fl oz / ½ cup beef stock

For the Pastry Crust

225 g / 8 oz / 2 cups self-raising flour

2.5 ml / ½ tsp salt

75 g / 3 oz / 6 tbsp cold butter, grated

150 ml / ¼ pint / ⅔ cup cold water

1 To make the pastry, sift the flour and salt into a bowl and stir in the butter. Add all of the water and stir with a knife to form a loose dough. Turn out onto a floured surface and press together without over working.

2 Brush a 1.2 litre / 2 pint / 5 cup pudding basin with oil or butter. Roll out the dough with a dusting of flour to form a 25 cm / 10 in circle. Cut out a quarter section and save for the lid. Line the basin and set aside.

3 Mix the beef, mushrooms, onion, flour and seasoning in a large bowl. Transfer to the lined basin, add the Worcestershire sauce and top up with the beef stock. Bring overlapping pastry edges towards the centre, moisten with water and cover the top with the leftover pastry.

4 Place a circle of greaseproof paper on the pastry, then cover the whole basin with a 46 cm / 18 in piece of foil. Boil 5 cm / 2 in of water in a pan and lower the basin into the pan. Cover and steam for 2½ hours, making sure the water doesn't boil away.

5 When ready to serve, turn out onto a plate and serve with curly kale, carrots and boiled potatoes.

Rich Beef Stew with Cep Dumplings

As if the temptation of a rich beef stew isn't enough, here it is crowned with cep dumplings.

SERVES 4

60 ml / 4 tbsp vegetable oil

900 g / 2 lb chuck steak, diced

150 ml / ¼ pint / ⅔ cup red wine

2 medium onions, halved and sliced

½ celery stick, chopped

450 g / 1 lb open cap wild or cultivated field mushrooms, sliced

½ garlic clove, crushed

600 ml / 1 pint / 2½ cups beef stock

30 ml / 2 tbsp tomato purée

10 ml / 2 tsp black olive purée

15 ml / 1 tbsp wine vinegar

5 ml / 1 tsp anchovy sauce

1 sprig thyme

salt and freshly ground black pepper

For the Cep Dumplings

275 g / 10 oz / 2¼ cups self-raising flour

2.5 ml / ½ tsp salt

115 g / 4 oz / ½ cup cold butter, finely diced

45 ml / 3 tbsp chopped fresh parsley

5 ml / 1 tsp chopped fresh thyme

dried ceps, soaked in warm water for 20 minutes

250 ml / 8 fl oz / 1 cup cold milk

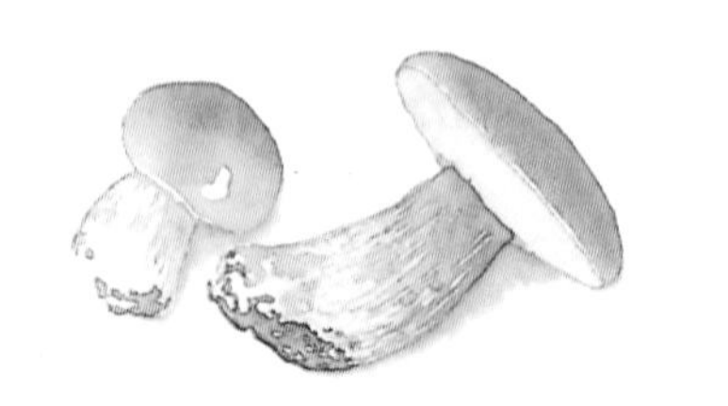

1 Preheat the oven to 170°C / 325°F / Gas 3. Season the meat with pepper then heat half of the oil in a pan, and seal the meat over a high heat. The liquid that appears must be evaporated before the meat will brown.

2 When the meat has browned, transfer to a flameproof casserole and pour off the fat from the pan. Add the wine to the pan and stir with a flat wooden spoon to loosen the sediment. Pour over the meat.

3 Wipe the pan clean then heat the remaining oil, add the onions and celery and brown lightly. Add to the casserole with the mushrooms, garlic, beef stock, tomato and olive purée, vinegar, anchovy sauce and thyme. Bring to a simmer, cover and cook in the oven for 1½–2 hours.

4 To make the dumplings, sift the flour and salt together, add the butter, then the parsley and thyme. Drain the ceps and chop finely. Add the ceps and milk to the mixture and stir with a knife to make a soft dough, taking care not to overmix.

5 Flour your hands and form the mixture into thumb-sized dumplings. Drop them into simmering water and cook uncovered for 10–12 minutes. When cooked, remove and arrange on top of the stew.

Braised Beef with Mushroom Gravy

Delicious gravy is an integral part of a good stew.

SERVES 4

900 g / 2 lb chuck steak, sliced

salt and freshly ground black pepper

60 ml / 4 tbsp vegetable oil

150 ml / ¼ pint / ⅔ cup red wine

2 medium onions, halved and sliced

½ celery stick, chopped

450 g / 1 lb open cap wild or cultivated field mushrooms, sliced

½ garlic clove, crushed

600 ml / 1 pint / 2½ cups beef stock

30 ml / 2 tbsp tomato purée

10 ml / 2 tsp black olive purée

5 ml / 1 tsp anchovy sauce

1 sprig thyme

15 ml / 1 tbsp wine vinegar

1 Preheat the oven to 170°C / 325°F / Gas 3. Season the meat with pepper. Heat half of the oil in a large frying pan, and seal the beef over a high heat. Liquid will appear, which must be evaporated before the meat will brown and take on flavour.

2 Transfer the meat to a flameproof casserole and pour off the fat from the pan. Return the pan to the heat, add the wine and stir briskly. Pour over the meat and wipe the pan clean.

3 Heat the remaining oil in the pan, add the onions and celery and brown lightly. Add the mushrooms, garlic, beef stock, tomato and olive purée, anchovy sauce and thyme to the casserole. Set over the heat and bring to a simmer. Cover and cook in the oven for about 2 hours until the meat is tender. Add the vinegar and adjust the seasoning. Serve with mashed potatoes, swede and cabbage.

Lamb Chop Sauté with a Sauce of Woodland Mushrooms

SERVES 4

4 × 175 g / 6 oz lamb chops
salt and freshly ground black pepper
30 ml / 2 tbsp olive oil
75 ml / 3 fl oz / ⅓ cup red wine
225 g / 8 oz assorted wild and cultivated mushrooms such as chanterelles, ceps, bay boletus, horn of plenty, saffron milk-caps, parasol mushrooms, oyster, Caesar's, St George's or field mushrooms, trimmed and sliced
½ garlic clove, crushed
200 ml / 7 fl oz / ⅞ cup chicken stock, boiling
10 ml / 2 tsp cornflour
5 ml / 1 tsp Dijon mustard
2.5 ml / ½ tsp black olive paste
5 ml / 1 tsp wine vinegar
25 g / 1 oz / 2 tbsp unsalted butter

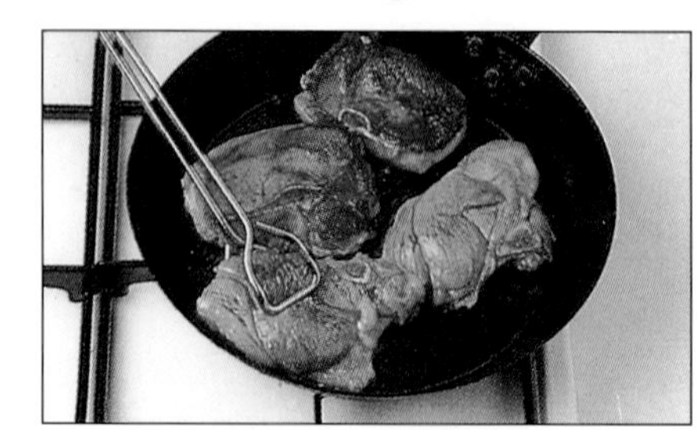

1 Season the lamb with black pepper, then moisten with 15 ml / 1 tbsp of the oil. Sauté over a steady heat for 6–8 minutes for medium-rare meat or 12–15 minutes for well done.

Cook's Tip
Do not season cut pieces of meat with salt before cooking. This can cause the meat to dry and toughen. Season before serving.

2 Transfer the lamb to a plate, cover and keep warm. Pour off any excess oil from the pan and heat the sediment until it browns. Add the red wine and stir with a flat wooden spoon to loosen the sediment. Add the mushrooms, stir briefly and then add the chicken stock and simmer for 3–4 minutes.

3 Place the cornflour, mustard and olive paste in a cup and blend with 15 ml / 1 tbsp cold water. Stir into the pan and simmer briefly to thicken. Add the vinegar, stir in the butter and season to taste. Season the lamb with a little salt, spoon the sauce over the top and serve with sautéed potatoes, French beans and carrots.

Black Pepper Beef Steaks with Red Wine and Mushroom Sauce

SERVES 4

4 × 225 g / 8 oz sirloin or rump steaks
15 ml / 1 tbsp black peppercorns, cracked
15 ml / 1 tbsp olive oil
120 ml / 4 fl oz / ½ cup red wine
225 g / 8 oz assorted wild and cultivated mushrooms such as ceps, bay boletus, chanterelles, horn of plenty, saffron milk-caps, blewits, morels, Paris mushrooms, field, oyster, Caesar's and St George's mushrooms or cauliflower fungus, trimmed and sliced
½ garlic clove, crushed
300 ml / ½ pint / 1¼ cups beef stock
15 ml / 1 tbsp cornflour
5 ml / 1 tsp Dijon mustard
10 ml / 2 tsp fish sauce (optional)
5 ml / 1 tsp wine vinegar
75 ml / 5 tbsp crème fraîche

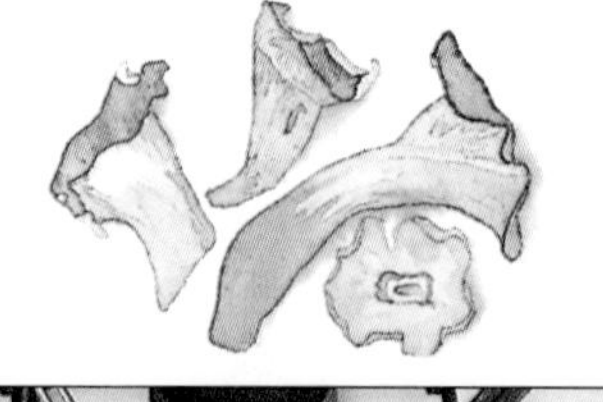

1 Place a large frying pan over a high heat. Season the steaks with cracked pepper and moisten with oil.

Cook's Tip
In terms of both flavour and tenderness, the best cut of steak is taken from the rump end. Rib steaks are also good, but because of their size, they are best suited to serve two.

2 Fry the steaks for 6–8 minutes for medium-rare meat, or 12–15 minutes for well done, turning once. Transfer to a plate and keep warm.

3 Pour off any excess fat, return the pan to the heat and brown the sediment. Add the wine and loosen the sediment with a flat wooden spoon. Add the mushrooms and garlic and soften for 6–8 minutes. Add the stock.

4 Place the cornflour and mustard in a cup and blend with 15 ml / 1 tbsp cold water. Stir into the pan juices and simmer to thicken. Add the fish sauce, if using, the vinegar, and the crème fraîche. Spoon the sauce over the steaks and scatter with parsley.

Beef Stroganoff with a Chantarelle Parsley Cream

This dish is believed to be named after a 19th century Russian diplomat, Count Paul Stroganoff. It was originally made with fillet steak, wild mushrooms and cream, but has suffered many changes. Here is an attempt at the original.

SERVES 4

450 g / 1 lb fillet or rump steak, trimmed and cut into thin strips

salt and freshly ground black pepper

30 ml / 2 tbsp olive oil

45 ml / 3 tbsp brandy

2 shallots, finely chopped

225 g / 8 oz chanterelle mushrooms, trimmed and halved

150 ml / ¼ pint / ⅔ cup beef stock

75 ml / 5 tbsp soured cream

5 ml / 1 tsp Dijon mustard

½ sweet gherkin, chopped

45 ml / 3 tbsp chopped fresh parsley

1 Season the steak with pepper, heat half of the oil in a pan and cook for 2 minutes. Transfer the meat to a plate.

Cook's Tip
If you can't afford fillet steak, buy best rump or sirloin.

2 Place the pan over a moderately high heat and brown the sediment. Stand back from the pan, add the brandy, tilt towards the flame (or ignite with a match if cooking on an electric hob) and burn off the alcohol vapour. Pour these juices over the meat, cover and keep warm.

3 Wipe the pan clean, heat the remaining oil and lightly brown the shallots. Add the mushrooms and fry gently for 3–4 minutes to soften.

4 Add the stock and simmer for a few minutes and then add the soured cream, mustard and gherkin together with the steak and its juices. Simmer briefly, season to taste and stir in the chopped parsley. Serve with buttered noodles dressed with poppy seeds.

Sauté of Pork with Jerusalem Artichokes and Horn of Plenty

The Jerusalem artichoke has an earthy quality not unlike the flavours of the horn of plenty.

SERVES 4

45 ml / 3 tbsp vegetable oil

1 medium onion, halved and sliced

1 celery stick, sliced

1 medium carrot, peeled, halved and sliced

675 g / 1½ lb lean pork, loin or thick end, cut into strips

45 ml / 3 tbsp plain flour

500 ml / 18 fl oz / 2¼ cups chicken stock

75 g / 3 oz Jerusalem artichokes, peeled and thickly sliced

115 g / 4 oz horn of plenty or winter chanterelles, trimmed

15 ml / 1 tbsp green olive paste

15 ml / 1 tbsp lemon juice

salt and freshly ground black pepper

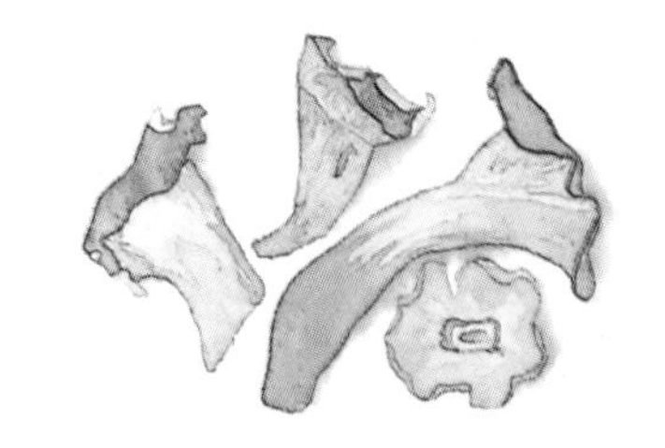

Cook's Tip

Jerusalem artichokes go a long way to provide richness to a dish. If used in excess, however, they sometimes cause flatulence.

1 Heat the oil in a heavy skillet or frying pan, add the onion, celery and carrot and fry gently for 6–8 minutes to soften.

2 Push the vegetables to one side of the pan, add the pork and seal. Stir in the flour and remove from the heat.

3 Add the stock gradually and stir so that the flour is completely absorbed by the stock.

4 Add the artichokes, mushrooms and olive paste and bring to a simmer. Cover with a lid or foil and cook very gently for about 1 hour. Add the lemon juice, adjust the seasoning and serve with a mixture of wild and long grain rice and petits pois.

Pork Sausage Puff with a Seam of Wild Mushrooms

Fresh pork sausages needn't be cooked in their skins. To make the most of them, remove the meat and wrap it in a puff pastry parcel. A thick seam of wild mushrooms gives a seasonal twist.

SERVES 4

50 g / 2 oz / 4 tbsp unsalted butter

½ garlic clove, crushed

15 ml / 1 tbsp chopped fresh thyme

450 g / 1 lb assorted wild and cultivated mushrooms such as ceps, bay boletus, chanterelles, horn of plenty, saffron milk-caps, blewits, chicken of the woods, oyster, field, Caesar's and St George's mushrooms, trimmed and sliced

50 g / 2 oz / 1 cup fresh white breadcrumbs

75 ml / 5 tbsp chopped fresh parsley

salt and freshly ground black pepper

350 g / 12 oz puff pastry, thawed if frozen

675 g / 1½ lb best pork sausages

1 egg, beaten with a pinch of salt

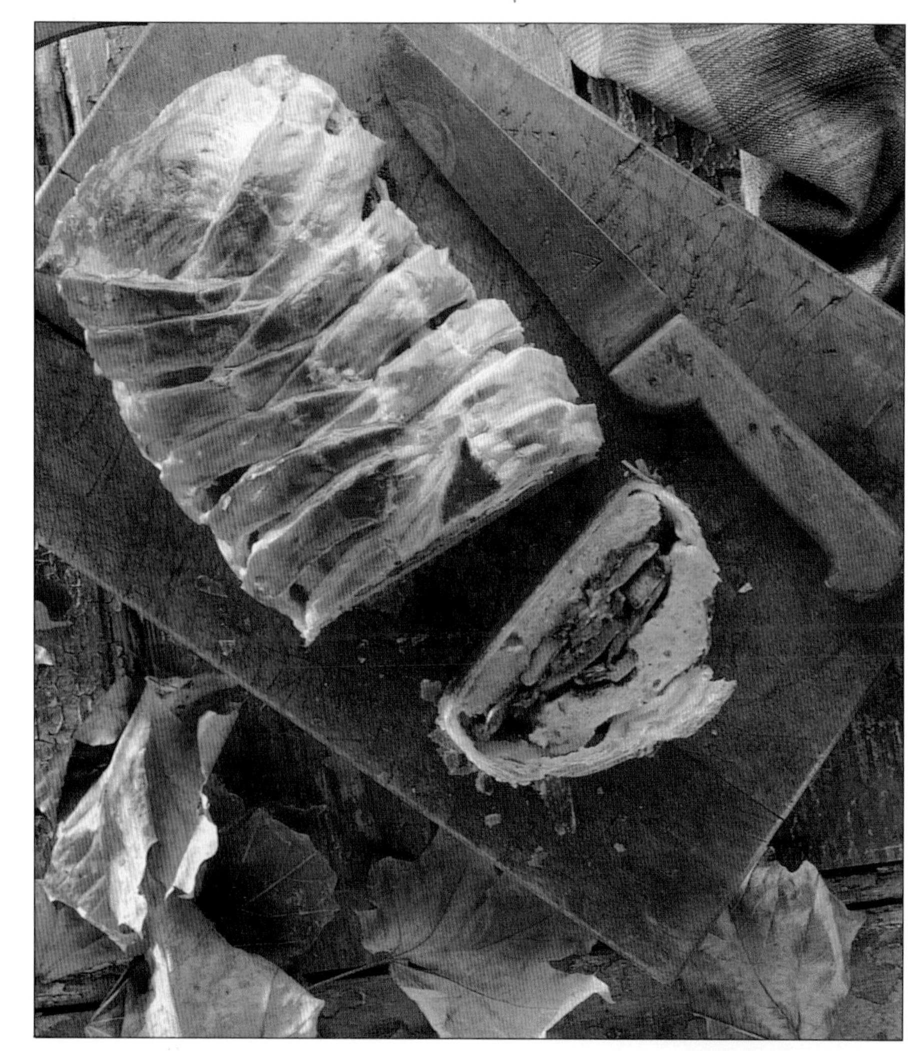

1 Preheat the oven to 180°C / 350°F / Gas 4. Melt the butter in a large non-stick frying pan, add the garlic, thyme and mushrooms and soften gently for 5–6 minutes. When the mushroom juices begin to run, increase the heat to evaporate the juices. When quite dry, stir in the breadcrumbs and chopped parsley and season well.

2 Roll out the pastry on a floured surface to form a 36 × 25 cm / 14 × 10 in rectangle and place on a large baking sheet.

3 Immerse the sausages in a bowl of water, pierce and pull off their skins. Place half of the sausagemeat in a 13 cm / 5 in strip along the centre of the pastry. Cover with mushrooms, then with another layer of sausagemeat.

4 Make a series of 2.5 cm / 1 in slanting cuts in the pastry each side of the filling. Fold the two ends of pastry over the filling, moisten the pastry with beaten egg and then cross the top with alternate strips of pastry from each side. Allow to rest for 40 minutes, brush with a little more egg and bake in the oven for 1 hour.

Cook's Tip

A good pinch of salt added to a beaten egg will break down and improve the finished glaze.

Coriander Lamb Kebabs with an Almond Chanterelle Sauce

The delicate sweetness of lamb combines well with apricot-scented chanterelles, used here to make this especially delicious almond sauce.

SERVES 4

8 lamb cutlets, trimmed
25 g / 1 oz / 2 tbsp unsalted butter
225 g / 8 oz chanterelle mushrooms, trimmed
25 g / 1 oz / ¼ cup whole almonds, toasted
50 g / 2 oz white bread, crusts removed
250 ml / 8 fl oz / 1 cup milk
45 ml / 3 tbsp olive oil
2.5 ml / ½ tsp caster sugar
10 ml / 2 tsp lemon juice
salt and cayenne pepper

For the Marinade

45 ml / 3 tbsp olive oil
15 ml / 1 tbsp lemon juice
10 ml / 2 tsp ground coriander
½ garlic clove, crushed
10 ml / 2 tsp clear honey

1 Mix all marinade ingredients together, pour over the lamb and leave for at least 30 minutes.

2 Fry the chanterelles gently in butter without colouring for 3–4 minutes. Set aside.

3 Place the almonds in a processor and grind finely. Add half of the chanterelles, the bread, milk, oil, sugar and lemon juice, then process.

4 Preheat a moderate grill. Thread the lamb onto four metal skewers, and cook for 6–8 minutes on each side. Season the sauce then spoon over the kebabs. Add the remaining chanterelles and serve with potatoes and a salad.

Cook's Tip

Almond chanterelle sauce makes a delicious dressing for pasta. Serve with a handful of chanterelles cooked in butter.

Beef Wellington made Rich with Mushrooms

There are two ways of preparing beef Wellington: both involve a length of fillet steak wrapped and baked in flaky pastry. Traditionally the beef is spread with a layer of goose liver pâté, but because of its high price, many cooks turn to an equally delicious and infinitely cheaper pâté of woodland mushrooms.

SERVES 4

675 g / 1½ lb fillet steak, tied
freshly ground black pepper
15 ml / 1 tbsp vegetable oil
350 g / 12 oz puff pastry, thawed if frozen
1 egg, beaten, to glaze

For the Parsley Pancakes

50 g / 2 oz / 5 tbsp plain flour
a pinch of salt
150 ml / ¼ pint / ⅔ cup milk
1 egg
30 ml / 2 tbsp chopped fresh parsley

For the Mushroom Pâté

25 g / 1 oz / 2 tbsp unsalted butter
2 shallots or 1 small onion, chopped
450 g / 1 lb assorted wild and cultivated mushrooms such as oyster mushrooms, ceps, bay boletus, orange birch bolete, shaggy ink caps, chanterelles, saffron milk caps, parasol mushrooms, blewits, closed field or St George's mushrooms, trimmed and chopped
50 g / 2 oz / 1 cup fresh white breadcrumbs
75 ml / 8 tbsp double cream
2 egg yolks

1 Preheat the oven to 220°C / 425°F / Gas 7. Season the fillet steak with several twists of black pepper. Heat the oil in a roasting tin, add the steak and quickly sear to brown all sides. Transfer to the oven and roast for 15 minutes for rare, 20 minutes for medium-rare or 25 minutes for well-done meat. Set aside to cool. Reduce the temperature to 190°C / 375°F / Gas 5.

2 To make the pancakes, beat the flour, salt, half the milk, the egg and parsley together until smooth, then stir in the remaining milk. Heat a greased, non-stick pan and pour in enough batter to coat the bottom. When set, turn over and cook the other side briefly until lightly browned. Continue with remaining batter – the recipe makes three or four.

3 To make the mushroom pâté, fry the shallots or onion in butter to soften without colouring. Add the mushrooms and cook until their juices begin to run. Increase the heat and cook briskly so that the juices evaporate. Combine the breadcrumbs with the cream and egg yolks. When the mushrooms are quite dry, add the bread and cream mixture and blend to make a smooth paste. Allow to cool.

Cook's Tip

Beef Wellington can be prepared up to 8 hours in advance but should be kept at room temperature as the meat will not heat through in the cooking times given if it is chilled before cooking begins. Instead of using a meat thermometer, you can insert a metal skewer into the meat. If the skewer is cold the meat is not done, if it is warm the meat is rare and if it is hot it is well-done.

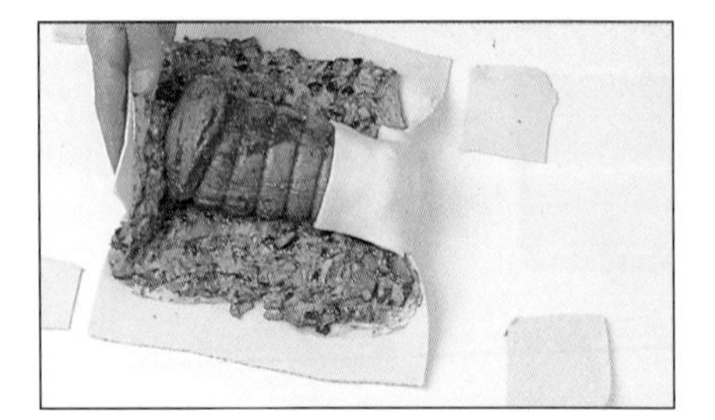

4 Roll out the pastry and cut into a rectangle 36 × 30 cm / 14 × 12 in. Place two pancakes on the pastry and spread with mushroom pâté. Place the beef on top and spread over any remaining pâté. Cover with the remaining pancakes. Cut out four squares from the corners of the pastry. Moisten the pastry edges with egg and then wrap them over the meat.

5 Decorate the top with the reserved pastry trimmings, transfer to a baking sheet and rest in a cool place until ready to cook.

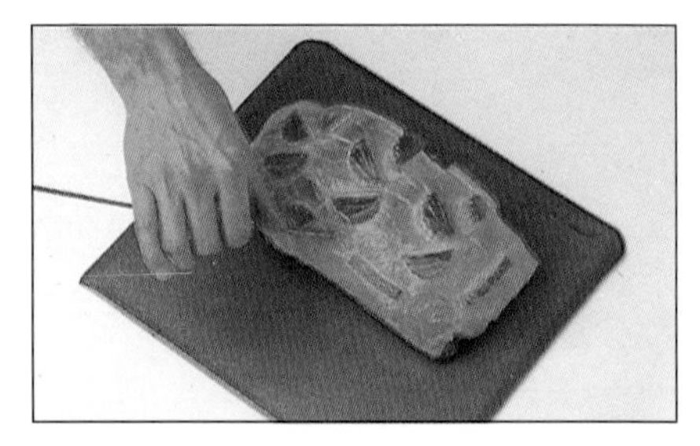

6 Brush evenly with beaten egg. Cook the Wellington for about 40 minutes until golden brown. To ensure that the meat is heated through, test with a meat thermometer. It should read 125–130°F (52–54°C) for rare, 135°C (57°F) for medium-rare and 160°C (71°F) for well-done meat.

Roast Leg of Lamb with a Wild Mushroom Stuffing

When the thigh bone is removed from a leg of lamb a stuffing can be put in its place. This not only makes the joint easier to carve but also gives an excellent flavour to the meat.

SERVES 4

1 × 1.8 kg / 4 lb leg of lamb, boned
salt and freshly ground black pepper

For the Wild Mushroom Stuffing

25 g / 1 oz / 2 tbsp butter, plus extra for gravy
1 shallot or 1 small onion
225 g / 8 oz assorted wild and cultivated mushrooms such as chanterelles, ceps, bay boletus, horn of plenty, blewits, oyster, St George's, field and Caesar's mushrooms, trimmed and chopped
½ garlic clove, crushed
1 sprig thyme, chopped
25 g / 1 oz crustless white bread, diced
2 egg yolks
salt and freshly ground black pepper

For the Wild Mushroom Gravy

50 ml / 3½ tbsp red wine
400 ml / 14 fl oz / 1⅔ cups chicken stock, boiling
5 g / ⅙ oz / 2 tbsp dried ceps, bay boletus or saffron milk-caps, soaked in boiling water for 20 minutes
20 ml / 4 tsp cornflour
5 ml / 1 tsp Dijon mustard
2.5 ml / ½ tsp wine vinegar
knob of butter
watercress, to garnish

1 Preheat the oven to 200°C / 400°F / Gas 6. To make the stuffing, melt the butter in a large non-stick frying pan and gently fry the shallot or onion without colouring. Add the mushrooms, garlic and thyme and stir until the mushrooms juices begin to run, then increase the heat so that they evaporate completely.

2 Transfer the mushrooms to a mixing bowl, add the bread, egg yolks and seasoning and mix well. Allow to cool slightly.

3 Season the inside cavity of the lamb and then press the stuffing into the cavity, using a spoon or your fingers. Tie up the end with fine string and then tie around the joint so that it does not lose its shape.

4 Place the lamb in a roasting tin and roast in the oven for 15 minutes per 450 g / 1 lb for rare meat and 20 minutes per 450 g / 1 lb for medium-rare. A 1.8 kg / 4 lb leg will take 1 hour 20 minutes if cooked medium-rare.

5 Transfer the lamb to a warmed serving plate, cover and keep warm. To make the gravy, spoon off all excess fat from the roasting tin and brown the sediment over a moderate heat. Add the wine and stir with a flat wooden spoon to loosen the sediment. Add the chicken stock, the mushrooms and their soaking liquid.

6 Place the cornflour and mustard in a cup and blend with 15 ml / 1 tbsp water. Stir into the stock and simmer to thicken. Add the vinegar. Season to taste, and stir in the butter. Garnish the lamb with watercress, and serve with roast potatoes, carrots and broccoli.

Cook's Tip

If you buy your meat from a butcher, ask for the thigh bone to be taken out.

Fish &
Shellfish

Shellfish Risotto with Fruits of the Forest

The creamy nature of short-grain rice cooked with onions and a simple stock provides the basis for this delicious combination of shellfish and mushrooms.

SERVES 4

45 ml / 3 tbsp olive oil

1 medium onion, chopped

225 g / 8 oz assorted wild and cultivated mushrooms such as ceps, bay boletus, chanterelles, chicken of the woods, saffron milk-caps, horn of plenty, wood blewits, oyster, St George's, Caesar's and truffles, trimmed and sliced

450 g / 1 lb / 2¼ cups short-grain Arborio or Carnaroli rice

1.2 litres / 2 pints / 5 cups chicken or vegetable stock, boiling

150 ml / ¼ pint / ⅔ cup white wine

115 g / 4 oz raw prawns, peeled

225 g / 8 oz live mussels

225 g / 8 oz Venus or carpet shell clams

1 medium squid, cleaned, trimmed and sliced

3 drops truffle oil (optional)

75 ml / 5 tbsp chopped fresh parsley and chervil

celery salt and cayenne pepper

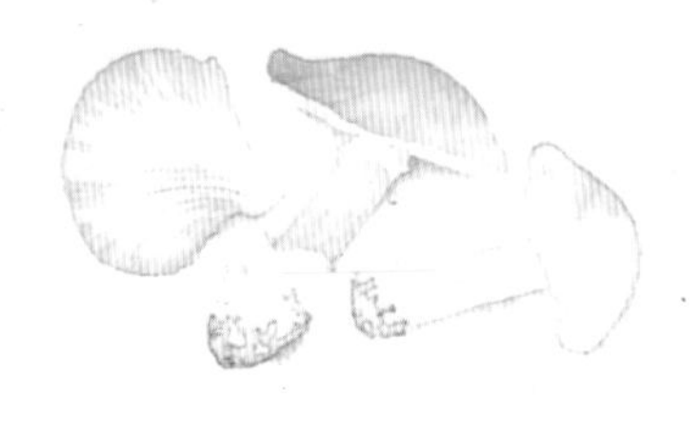

1 Heat the oil in a large skillet and fry the onion for 6–8 minutes until soft but not brown.

3 Pour in the stock and wine. Add the prawns, mussels, clams and squid, stir and simmer for 15 minutes.

2 Add the mushrooms and soften until their juices begin to run. Stir in the rice and heat through.

4 Add the truffle oil if using, stir in the herbs, cover and stand for 5–10 minutes. Season to taste with celery salt and a pinch of cayenne pepper and serve with open-textured bread.

Cook's Tip

Before cooking, scrub the mussels and clams, then tap them with a knife. If any of the shells do not close, discard them. After cooking (see step 3), if any of the shells have not opened discard them too.

Deep Sea Scallops in a Forest of Wild Mushrooms

From the depths of the sea and forest come two flavours that marry perfectly in a smooth creamy sauce.

SERVES 4

350 g / 12 oz puff pastry, thawed if frozen
1 egg, beaten, to glaze
75 g / 3 oz / 6 tbsp unsalted butter
12 scallops, trimmed and thickly sliced
salt and freshly ground black pepper
2 shallots, chopped
½ stick celery, cut into strips
½ medium carrot, peeled and cut into strips
225 g / 8 oz assorted wild mushrooms, such as chanterelles, chicken of the woods, cauliflower fungus, oyster, Caesar's and St George's mushrooms, trimmed and sliced
60 ml / 4 tbsp Noilly Prat or other dry vermouth
150 ml / ¼ pint / ⅔ cup crème fraîche
4 egg yolks
15 ml / 1 tbsp lemon juice
celery salt and cayenne pepper

1 Roll the pastry out on a floured surface, cut into four 13 cm / 5 in circles, and then trim into shell shapes. Brush with a little beaten egg and mark a shell pattern on each with a small knife. Place on a baking sheet, chill and rest for 1 hour. Preheat the oven to 200°C / 400°F / Gas 6.

2 Melt 25 g / 1 oz / 2 tbsp of the butter in a pan, season the scallops and cook for not longer than 30 seconds over a high heat. Transfer to a plate.

3 Bake the pastry shapes for 20–25 minutes until golden and quite dry. Fry the shallots, celery and carrots gently in the remaining butter without colouring. Add the mushrooms and cook over a moderate heat until the juices begin to run. Pour in the vermouth and increase the heat to evaporate the juices.

4 Add the crème fraîche and cooked scallops and bring to a simmer (do not boil). Remove the pan from the heat and blend in the egg yolks. Return the pan to a gentle heat and cook for a moment or two until the sauce has thickened to the consistency of thin cream, remove the pan from the heat. Season and add the lemon juice.

5 Split the pastry shapes open and place on four plates. Spoon in the filling and replace the tops. Serve with potatoes and salad.

Cook's Tip

Take care not to use dark mushrooms in a cream sauce.

Fillets of Trout with a Spinach and Field Mushroom Sauce

Many people like the idea of trout, but have trouble getting it off the bone. Trout fillets are the answer to this problem and taste delicious with a rich spinach and mushroom sauce.

SERVES 4

4 brown or rainbow trout, filleted and skinned to make 8 fillets

For the Spinach and Mushroom Sauce

75 g / 3 oz / 6 tbsp unsalted butter

¼ medium onion, chopped

225 g / 8 oz closed field or horse mushrooms, chopped

300 ml / ½ pint / 1¼ cups chicken stock, boiling

225 g / 8 oz frozen chopped spinach

10 ml / 2 tsp cornflour

150 ml / ¼ pint / ⅔ cup crème fraîche

salt and freshly ground black pepper

grated nutmeg

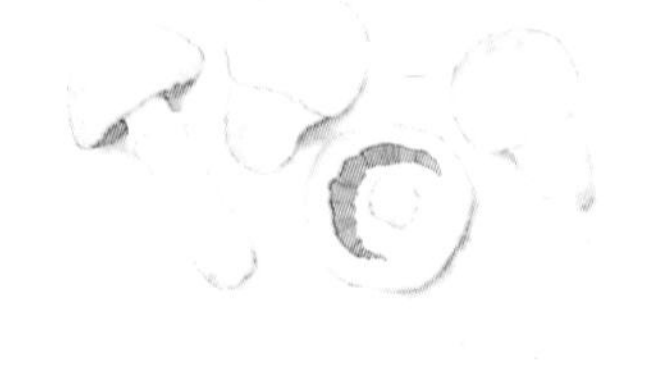

1 To make the sauce, melt 50 g / 2 oz / 4 tbsp of the butter in a frying pan and fry the onion until soft. Add the mushrooms and cook until the juices begin to run. Add the stock and the spinach and cook until the spinach has completely thawed.

2 Blend the cornflour with 15 ml / 1 tbsp of cold water and stir into the mushroom mixture. Simmer gently to thicken.

3 Liquidize the sauce until smooth, add the crème fraîche and season to taste with salt and pepper and a pinch of nutmeg. Turn into a serving jug and keep warm.

4 Melt the remaining butter in a large non-stick frying pan. Season the trout and cook for 6 minutes, turning once. Serve with new potatoes and young carrots with the sauce either poured over or served separately.

Cook's Tip

Spinach and mushroom sauce is also good with fillets of cod, haddock and sole.

Puff Pastry Salmon with a Chanterelle Cream Filling

The flavour of farmed salmon is helped by a creamy layer of chanterelle mushrooms.

SERVES 6

2 × 350 g / 12 oz puff pastry, thawed if frozen
1 egg, beaten, to glaze
2 large salmon fillets, about 900 g / 2 lb total weight, skinned and boned
375 ml / 13 fl oz / 1⅝ cups dry white wine
1 small carrot
1 small onion, halved
½ celery stick, chopped
1 sprig thyme

For the Chanterelle Cream

25 g / 1 oz / 2 tbsp unsalted butter
2 shallots, chopped
225 g / 8 oz chanterelles or saffron milk-caps, trimmed and sliced
75 ml / 5 tbsp white wine
150 ml / ¼ pint / ⅔ cup double cream
45 ml / 3 tbsp chopped fresh chervil
30 ml / 2 tbsp chopped fresh chives

For the Hollandaise Sauce

175 g / 6 oz / ¾ cup unsalted butter
2 egg yolks
10 ml / 2 tsp lemon juice
salt and freshly ground black pepper

1 Preheat the oven to 200°C / 400°F / Gas 6. Roll out the pastry on a floured surface to form a rectangle 10 cm / 4 in longer and 5 cm / 2 in wider than the fillets. Trim into a fish shape, decorate with a pastry cutter and glaze with beaten egg. Chill for 1 hour and then bake for 30–35 minutes until well risen and golden. Remove from the oven and split open horizontally. Reduce the oven temperature to 170°C / 325°F / Gas 3.

2 To make the chanterelle cream, fry the shallots gently in butter until soft but not coloured. Add the mushrooms and cook until their juices begin to run. Pour in the wine, increase the heat and evaporate the juices. When dry, add the cream and herbs and bring to a simmer. Season well, transfer to a bowl, cover and keep warm.

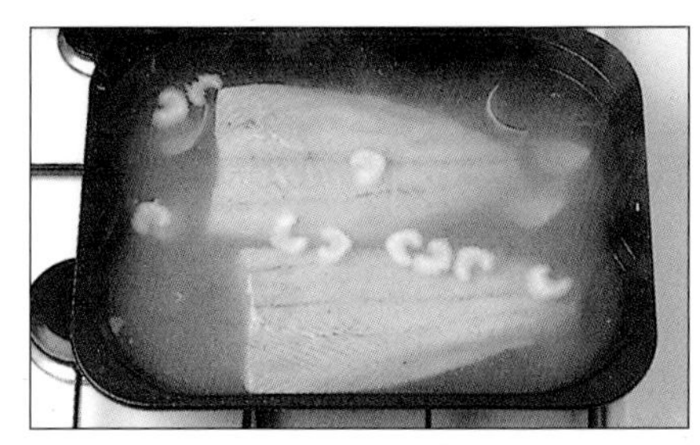

3 To poach the salmon fillet, place in a fish kettle or roasting tin. Add the wine, carrot, onion, celery, thyme and enough water to cover the fish. Bring to the boil slowly. As soon as the water begins to tremble, remove from the heat, cover and allow the fish to cook in this gentle heat for 30 minutes.

4 To make the sauce, melt the butter, skim the surface of any scum and pour into a jug, leaving behind the milky residue. Place the yolks and 15 ml / 1 tbsp of water in a glass bowl and place over a pan of simmering water. Whisk the yolks until thick and foamy. Remove from the heat and very slowly pour in the butter, whisking all the time. Add the lemon juice and season.

5 Place one salmon fillet on the base of the pastry, spread with the chanterelle cream and cover with the second fillet. Cover with the top of the pastry "fish" and warm through in the oven for about 10–15 minutes. Serve with the sauce.

Wild Mushroom and Cep Cockle Puffs

This dish is as much a soup as it is a fish course. Oyster mushrooms, ceps and cockles combine in a rich herb broth which is covered with pastry. When baked, the broth produces steam and the pastry puffs in a dome.

SERVES 4

350 g / 12 oz puff pastry, thawed, if frozen

1 egg beaten, to glaze

45 ml / 3 tbsp sesame seeds or celery seed

For the Soup

25 g / 1 oz / 2 tbsp unsalted butter

4 spring onions, trimmed and chopped

1 celery stick, sliced

1 small carrot, peeled, halved and sliced

115 g / 4 oz fresh young ceps or bay boletus, sliced

175 g / 6 oz oyster mushrooms

450 ml / ¾ pint / 1⅞ cup full-fat milk

275 g / 10 oz shelled fresh cockles, cooked

50 g / 2 oz samphire, trimmed (optional)

115 g / 4 oz cooked potato, diced

4 sprigs thyme

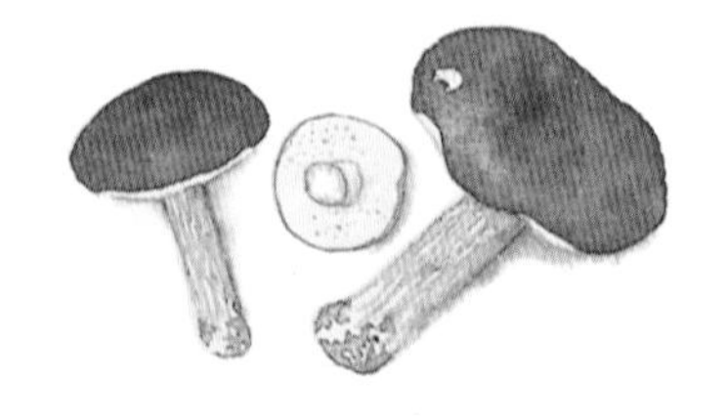

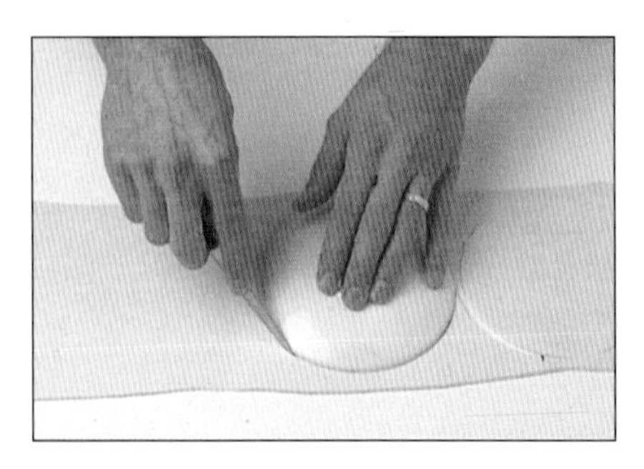

1 Roll out the pastry on a floured surface and cut into four 18 cm / 7 in rounds. Rest in a cool place for 1 hour. Preheat the oven to 190°C / 375°F / Gas 5.

2 Fry the spring onions, celery and carrot in butter for 2–3 minutes. Add the mushrooms and soften until the juices begin to flow. Transfer to a large saucepan.

3 Pour the milk over the mushrooms and bring to a simmer. Add the cockles, samphire and diced potato.

4 Heat through the contents of the saucepan and then ladle into four deep ovenproof soup bowls. Add a sprig of thyme to each.

5 Moisten the edges of the bowls with beaten egg, cover with the pastry rounds and firm the edges to seal. Brush with more beaten egg, sprinkle with sesame seeds and bake in the oven for 35–40 minutes until the pastry top is puffed and golden.

Cook's Tip

If fresh ceps are unavailable use closed button or Paris mushrooms.

Fresh Tuna Shiitake Teriyaki

Teriyaki is a sweet soy marinade usually used to glaze meat. Here Teriyaki enhances fresh tuna steaks served with rich shiitake mushrooms.

SERVES 4

4 × 175 g / 6 oz fresh tuna or yellow tail steaks

salt

150 ml / ¼ pint / ⅔ cup Teriyaki sauce

175 g / 6 oz shiitake mushrooms, sliced

225 g / 8 oz white radish, peeled

2 large carrots, peeled

1 Season the tuna steaks with a sprinkling of salt, then set aside for 20 minutes for it to penetrate. Pour the Teriyaki sauce over the fish and mushrooms and marinate for a further 20–30 minutes or for longer if you have the time.

Cook's Tip
One of the finest Teriyaki sauces is made by Kikkoman and can be found in most large supermarkets.

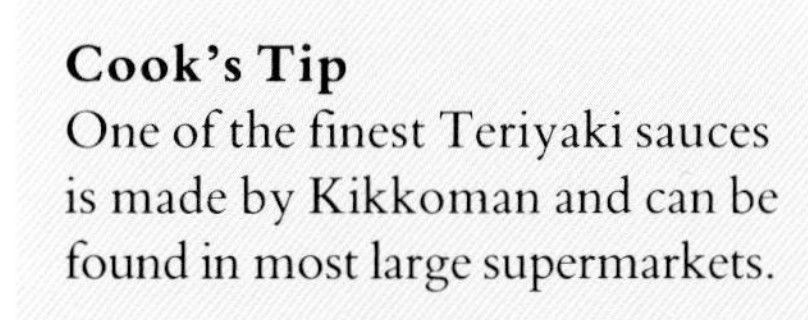

2 Preheat a moderate grill or barbecue. Remove the tuna from marinade and reserve the marinade. Cook the tuna for 8 minutes, turning once.

3 Transfer the mushrooms and marinade to a stainless steel saucepan and simmer for 3–4 minutes.

4 Slice the radish and carrot thinly, then shred finely with a chopping knife. Arrange in heaps on four serving plates and add the fish, with the mushrooms and sauce poured over. Serve with plain boiled rice.

Turbans of Lemon Sole with a Paris Mushroom Twist

The Paris mushroom *champignon de Paris* or chestnut mushroom is the French equivalent of the English white button mushroom. Its mild woodland flavour goes well with the lemon sole.

SERVES 4

900 g / 2 lb lemon sole, filleted and skinned to yield 450 g / 1 lb of fish

75 ml / 5 tbsp dry white wine

120 ml / 4 fl oz / ½ cup water

50 ml / 3½ tbsp double cream

10 ml / 2 tsp cornflour

10 ml / 2 tsp lemon juice

celery salt and cayenne pepper

For the Mushroom Filling

50 g / 2 oz / 4 tbsp unsalted butter, plus extra for greasing

1 shallot, finely chopped

175 g / 6 oz Paris or oyster mushrooms, finely chopped

15 ml / 1 tbsp chopped fresh thyme

salt and freshly ground black pepper

1 Preheat the oven to 190°C / 375°F / Gas 5 and butter an ovenproof dish. Make the mushroom filling. Melt the butter in a frying pan and fry the shallot until soft.

2 Add the mushrooms and thyme and cook until dry. Transfer to a bowl, season and allow to cool.

3 Lay the fish skin side uppermost, season and spread with the filling. Roll up each fillet, then place in the buttered dish.

4 Pour in the wine and water, cover with a piece of buttered greaseproof paper and cook in the oven for 20 minutes.

5 Transfer the fish to a warmed serving platter and strain the cooking juices into a small saucepan. Add the cream and bring to a simmer.

6 Blend the cornflour with 15 ml / 1 tbsp of water, add to the pan, stir and simmer to thicken, then add the lemon juice and season with celery salt and a pinch of cayenne pepper. Pour the sauce around the fish and serve with new potatoes, beans and carrots.

Cook's Tip

If planning ahead, the fish can be rolled and kept ready to cook for up to 8 hours.

Truffle and Lobster Risotto

To capture the precious qualities of the fresh truffle, partner it with lobster and serve in a silky smooth risotto. Both truffle shavings and truffle oil are added towards the end of cooking to preserve their flavour.

SERVES 4

50 g / 2 oz / 4 tbsp unsalted butter

1 medium onion, chopped

400 g / 14 oz / 2 cups Arborio or Carnaroli rice

1 sprig thyme

1.2 litres / 2 pints / 5 cups chicken stock

150 ml / ¼ pint / ⅔ cup dry white wine

1 freshly cooked lobster

45 ml / 3 tbsp chopped fresh parsley and chervil

3–4 drops truffle oil

2 hard-boiled eggs, sliced

1 fresh black or white truffle

1 Melt the butter in a large shallow pan, add the onion and fry gently until soft without letting it colour. Add the rice and thyme and stir well to coat evenly with fat. Pour in the chicken stock and wine, stir once and cook uncovered for 15 minutes.

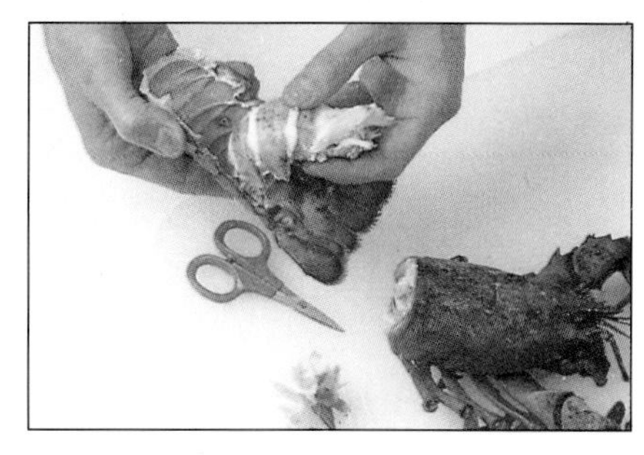

2 Twist off the lobster tail, cut the underside with scissors and remove white tail meat. Slice half of the meat then roughly chop the remainder. Break open the claws with a small hammer and remove the flesh, in one piece if possible.

3 Remove the rice from the heat, stir in the chopped lobster meat, herbs and truffle oil. Cover and leave to stand for 5 minutes.

4 Divide among warmed dishes and arrange the lobster and hard-boiled egg slices and shavings of fresh truffle on top. Serve immediately.

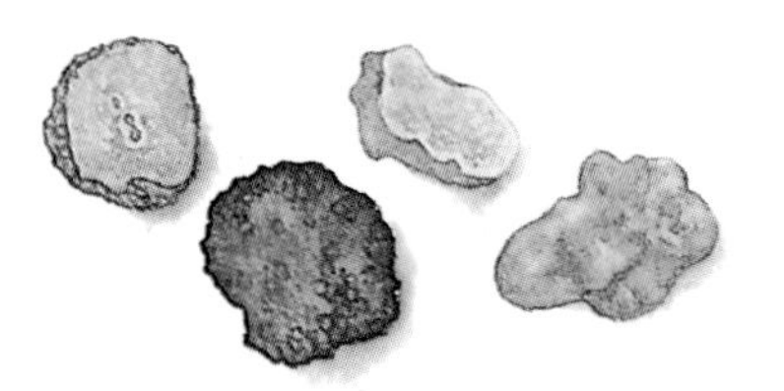

Cook's Tip

To make the most of the aromatic truffle scent, keep the tuber in the rice jar for a few days. Alternatively store with the eggs at room temperature.

Creamy Fish and Mushroom Pie

Fish pie is a healthy and hearty dish for a hungry family. To help the fish go further, mushrooms provide both flavour and nourishment.

SERVES 4

225 g / 8 oz assorted wild and cultivated mushrooms such as oyster, button, chanterelle or St George's mushrooms, trimmed and quartered

675 g / 1½ lb cod or haddock fillet, skinned and diced

600 ml / 1 pint / 2½ cups milk, boiling

For the Topping

900 g / 2 lb floury potatoes, peeled and quartered

25 g / 1 oz / 2 tbsp butter

150 ml / ¼ pint / ⅔ cup milk

salt and freshly ground black pepper

grated nutmeg

For the Sauce

50 g / 2 oz / 4 tbsp unsalted butter

1 medium onion, chopped

½ celery stick, chopped

50 g / 2 oz / ½ cup plain flour

10 ml / 2 tsp lemon juice

45 ml / 3 tbsp chopped fresh parsley

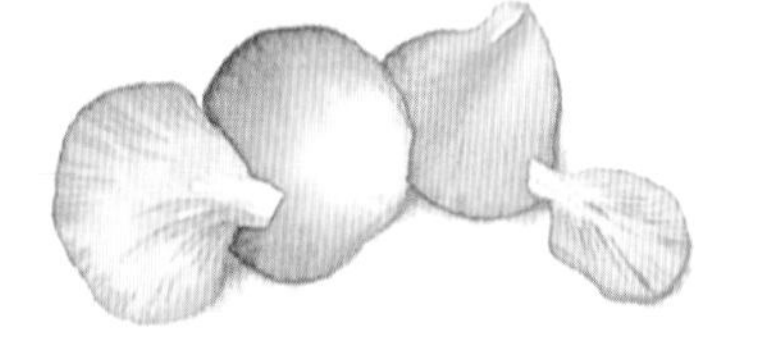

1 Preheat the oven to 200 °C / 400°F / Gas 6. Butter an ovenproof dish, scatter the mushrooms in the bottom, add the fish and season with salt and pepper. Pour on the boiling milk, cover and cook in the oven for 20 minutes. Using a slotted spoon, transfer the fish and mushrooms to a 1.5 litre / 2½ pint / 6¼ cup baking dish. Pour the poaching liquid into a jug and set aside.

2 Cover the potatoes with cold water, add a good pinch of salt and boil for 20 minutes. Drain and mash with the butter and milk. Season well.

3 To make the sauce, melt the butter in a saucepan, add the onion and celery and fry until soft but not coloured. Stir in the flour, then remove from the heat.

4 Slowly add the reserved liquid, stirring until absorbed. Return to the heat, stir and simmer to thicken. Add the lemon juice and parsley, season, then add to the baking dish.

5 Top with the mashed potato and return to the oven for 30–40 minutes until golden brown.

Pan-fried Salmon with a Tarragon Mushroom Sauce

Tarragon has a distinctive aniseed flavour that is good with fish, cream and mushrooms. This recipe uses oyster mushrooms to provide both texture and flavour.

SERVES 4

50 g / 2 oz / 4 tbsp unsalted butter

salt and cayenne pepper

4 × 175 g / 6 oz salmon steaks

1 shallot, finely chopped

175 g / 6 oz assorted wild and cultivated mushrooms such as oyster mushrooms, saffron milk-caps, bay boletus or cauliflower fungus, trimmed and sliced

200 ml / 7 fl oz / 7/8 cup chicken or vegetable stock

10 ml / 2 tsp cornflour

2.5 ml / 1/2 tsp mustard

50 ml / 3 1/2 tbsp crème fraîche

45 ml / 3 tbsp chopped fresh tarragon

5 ml / 1 tsp white wine vinegar

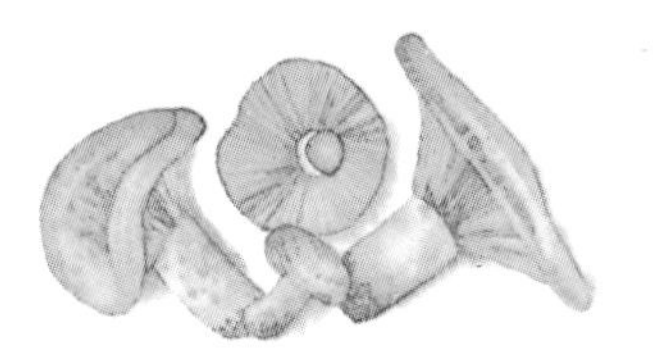

1 Melt half of the butter in a large non-stick frying pan, season the salmon and cook over a moderate heat for 8 minutes, turning once. Transfer to a plate, cover and keep warm.

2 Heat the remaining butter in the pan and gently fry the shallot to soften without letting it colour. Add the mushrooms and cook until the juices begin to flow. Add the stock and simmer for 2–3 minutes.

3 Put the cornflour and mustard in a cup and blend with 15 ml / 1 tbsp of water. Stir into the mushroom mixture and bring to a simmer, stirring, to thicken. Add the cream, tarragon, vinegar and salt and cayenne pepper.

4 Spoon the mushrooms over each salmon steak and serve with new potatoes and a green salad.

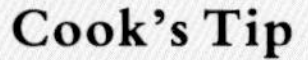

Cook's Tip

Fresh tarragon will bruise and darken quickly after chopping, so prepare the herb as and when you need it.

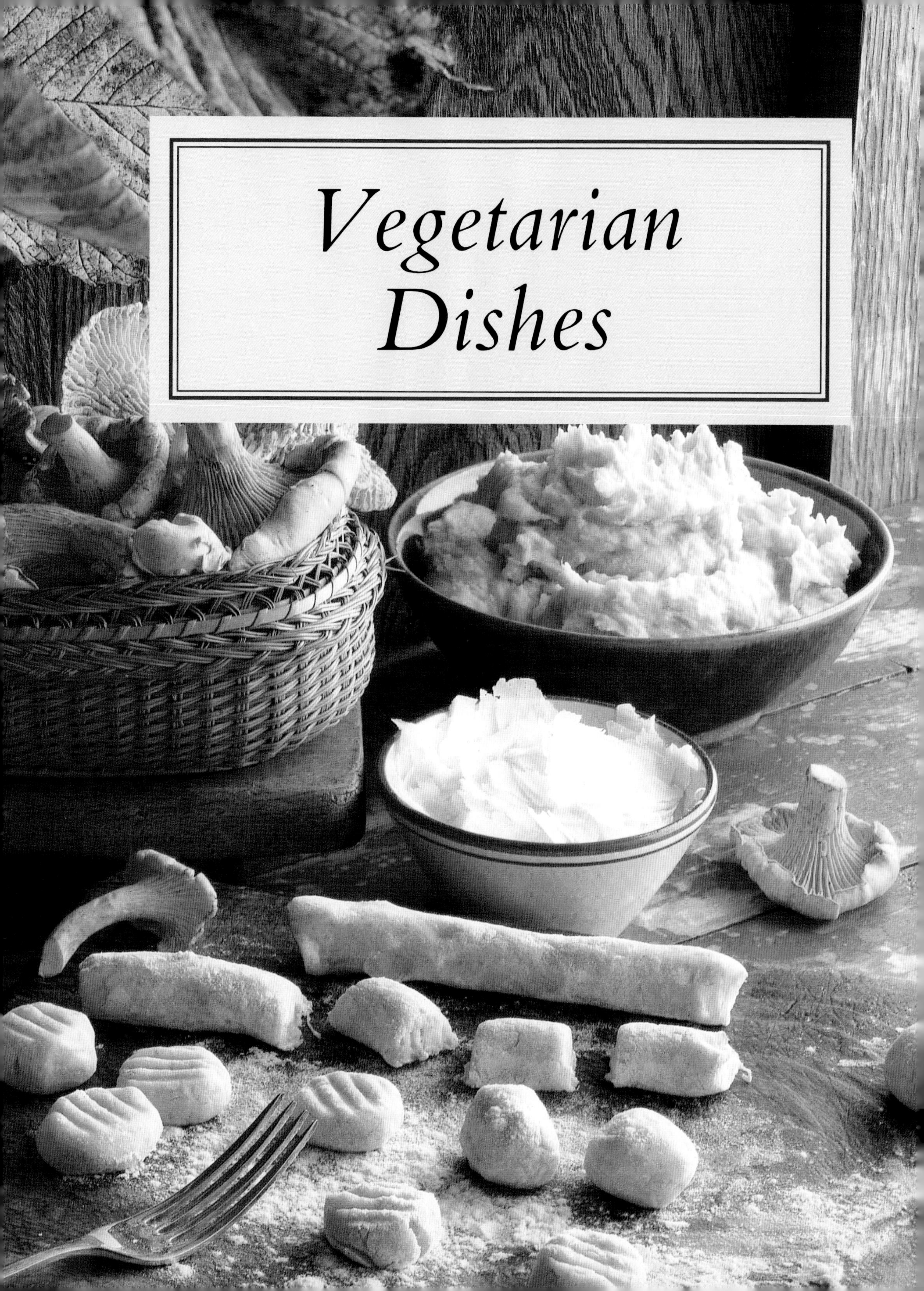

Vegetarian Dishes

Mushrooms in a Tarragon Cream Sauce

When your search for wild mushrooms yields only a few specimens and you have to provide breakfast for the proverbial five thousand, combine what you have with a few cultivated mushrooms – enhanced here in a creamy tarragon sauce.

SERVES 4

50 g / 2 oz / 4 tbsp unsalted butter, plus extra for spreading

2 shallots, finely chopped

50 g–225 g / 2–8 oz wild mushrooms such as St George's or Caesar's mushrooms, chanterelles, winter chanterelles, ceps, chicken of the woods, parasol mushrooms or hedgehog fungus, trimmed and sliced

350 g / 12 oz Paris mushrooms, trimmed and sliced

150 ml / 1/4 pint / 2/3 cup double cream

45 ml / 3 tbsp chopped fresh tarragon

4 slices brown or white bread

1 Melt the butter in a large non-stick frying pan, add the shallots and fry over a gentle heat until they are soft, without letting them colour.

Cook's Tip
Almost any variety of mushrooms can be used in a cream sauce, but do avoid dark specimens which can turn the sauce grey.

2 Add your chosen mushrooms and cook over a moderate heat to soften. Add the cream and tarragon, increase the heat and cook until thick and creamy.

3 Toast the bread and spread with butter. Spoon over the mushroom mixture and serve at once.

Saffron Milk-caps with Parsley, Butter and Pine Nuts

Serving wild mushrooms on toast is a quick, easy way to appreciate their individual flavours. Butter-fried saffron milk-caps are good, served with a handful of chopped parsley and a scattering of toasted pine nuts.

SERVES 4

25 g / 1 oz / 1/4 cup pine nuts

5 ml / 1 tsp vegetable oil

50 g / 2 oz / 4 tbsp unsalted butter, plus extra for spreading

1 shallot, finely chopped

350 g / 12 oz saffron milk-caps, trimmed and sliced

45 ml / 3 tbsp double cream

75 ml / 5 tbsp chopped fresh parsley

salt and freshly ground black pepper

4 slices brown or white bread

1 Fry the pine nuts in the oil, tilting the pan, and brown over a moderate heat. Set aside.

2 Soften the shallot in half the butter. Add the mushrooms and remaining butter and cook until soft. Stir in the cream and cook until thick. Stir in the parsley and season to taste.

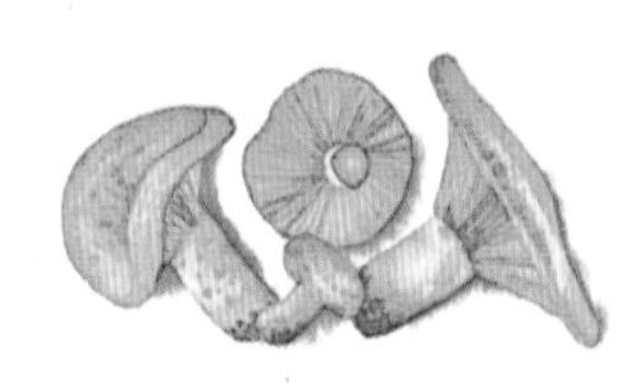

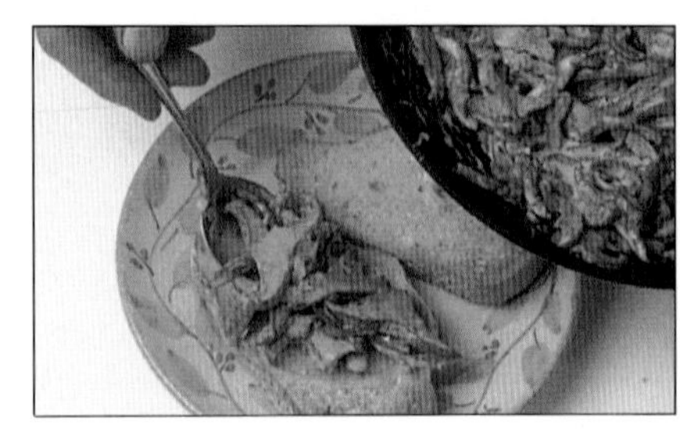

3 Toast the bread and spread with butter. Spoon the mushroom mixture over the toast, scatter with toasted pine nuts and serve.

Cook's Tip
Saffron milk-caps have hollow stems which can harbour insect larvae. Be sure to avoid any that are infested.

Toasted Brioche, Scrambled Eggs and Morels

Morels have a rich flavour that combines well with other rich ingredients such as eggs, cream and Madeira. This simple breakfast dish can be made with fresh or dried morels.

SERVES 4

150 g / 5 oz fresh morels or 15 g / ½ oz / ¼ cup dried

25 g / 1 oz / 2 tbsp unsalted butter

1 shallot, finely chopped

60 ml / 4 tbsp Madeira

60 ml / 4 tbsp crème fraîche

4 small brioches

For the Scrambled Eggs

8 eggs

60 ml / 4 tbsp crème fraîche

salt and freshly ground black pepper

25 g / 1 oz / 2 tbsp unsalted butter

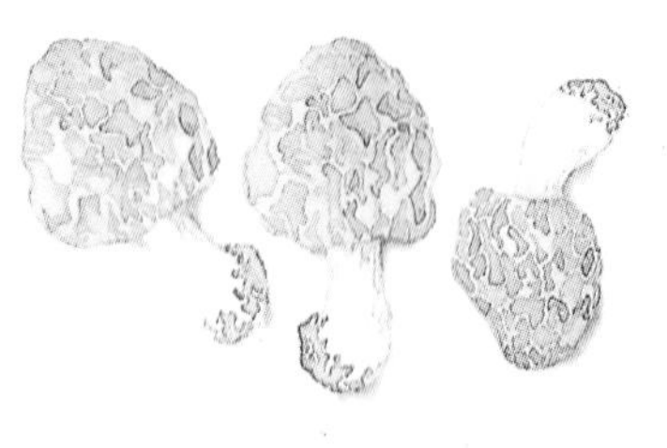

1 If using dried morels, cover with warm water, soak for 20 minutes and drain. Melt the butter in a non-stick frying pan and gently fry the shallot until it is softened. Add the morels and cook briefly, then stir in the Madeira and cook until the liquid is syrupy. Stir in the crème fraîche and simmer briefly. Season, transfer to a bowl and keep warm.

2 Remove the tops from the brioches and toast under a moderate grill.

Cook's Tip
Madeira provides an oaky hazelnut flavour to balance stronger-tasting mushrooms. You can also use a medium dry sherry.

3 Break the eggs into a jug, add the crème fraîche, season and beat with a fork. Melt the butter in the frying pan, pour in the eggs and cook, stirring gently but continuously until the eggs are slightly cooked. Remove from the heat: the eggs will continue cooking in their own heat.

4 Spoon the scrambled eggs over the brioches and top with morels.

English Muffins with a Florentine Parasol Topping

The parasol mushroom is prized for its delicate texture and rich flavour. The stems of open specimens are tough but both the stem and cap of closed parasols are delicious with a creamy spinach topping.

SERVES 4

400 g / 14 oz young leaf spinach, stems removed

salt and freshly ground black pepper

350 g / 12 oz parasol mushroom caps

50 g / 2 oz / 4 tbsp unsalted butter, plus extra for spreading

½ garlic clove, crushed

5 sprigs thyme

200 ml / 7 fl oz / 1 cup crème fraîche

pinch of grated nutmeg

4 English muffins, split

1 Rinse the spinach in plenty of water, then place in a large saucepan with a pinch of salt. Cover and cook over a steady heat for 6–8 minutes, then drain in a colander, pressing out as much water as you can with the back of a spoon. Chop the spinach finely.

2 Chop the mushrooms very finely, then melt the butter in a frying pan and add the mushrooms together with the garlic and 1 sprig of thyme. Cook for 3–4 minutes then add the chopped spinach and 150 ml / ¼ pint / ⅔ cup of the crème fraîche. Season with salt, pepper and a pinch of nutmeg. Toast the muffins, split and spread lightly with butter.

3 Spoon the spinach mixture onto the muffins, top with the remaining crème fraîche and garnish with thyme.

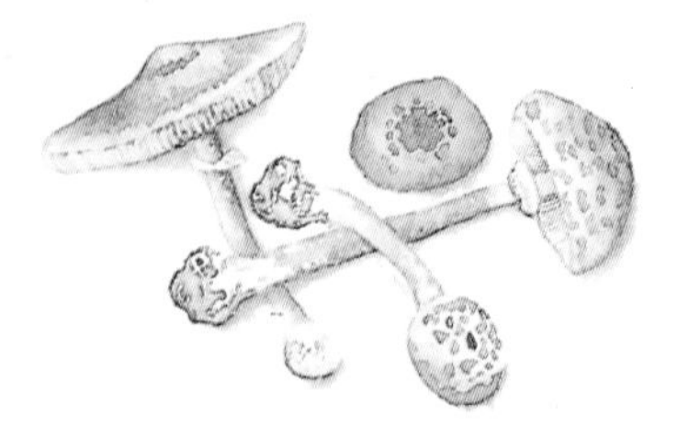

Cook's Tip
If using frozen chopped spinach, allow half the weight of fresh spinach, thaw thoroughly and squeeze dry.

Mushroom Picker's Omelette

Enthusiastic mushroom pickers have been known to carry with them a portable gas stove, an omelette pan and a few eggs, ready to assemble an on-site brunch.

SERVES 1

25 g / 1 oz / 2 tbsp unsalted butter, plus extra for cooking

115 g / 4 oz assorted wild and cultivated mushrooms such as young ceps, bay boletus, chanterelles, saffron milk-caps, closed field mushrooms, oyster mushrooms, hedgehog and St George's mushrooms, trimmed and sliced

3 eggs, at room temperature

salt and freshly ground black pepper

Cook's Tip
From start to finish, an omelette should be cooked and on the table in less than a minute. For best results use free range eggs at room temperature.

1 Melt the butter in a small omelette pan, add the mushrooms and cook until the juices run. Season, remove from pan and set aside. Wipe the pan.

2 Break the eggs into a bowl, season and beat with a fork. Heat the omelette pan over a high heat, add a knob of butter and let it begin to brown. Pour in the beaten egg and stir briskly with the back of a fork.

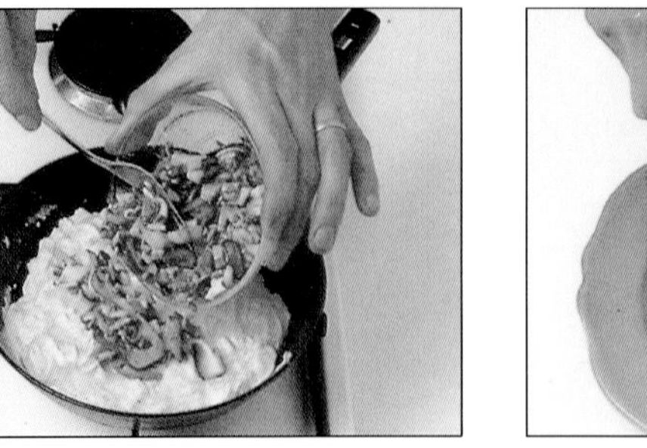

3 When the eggs are two-thirds scrambled, add the mushrooms and let the omelette finish cooking for 10–15 seconds.

4 Tap the handle of the omelette pan sharply with your fist to loosen the omelette from the pan then fold and turn onto a plate. Serve with warm crusty bread and a simple green salad.

Pumpkin Gnocchi with a Chanterelle Parsley Cream

Gnocchi is an Italian pasta dumpling usually made from potatoes, in this special recipe, pumpkin is added, too. A chanterelle sauce provides both richness and flavour.

SERVES 4

450 g / 1 lb peeled floury potatoes
450 g / 1 lb peeled pumpkin, chopped
2 egg yolks
200 g / 7 oz / 1¾ cups plain flour, plus more if necessary
pinch of ground allspice
1.5 ml / ¼ tsp ground cinnamon
pinch of grated nutmeg
finely grated rind of ½ orange
salt and freshly ground pepper

For the Sauce

30 ml / 2 tbsp olive oil
1 shallot
175 g / 6 oz fresh chanterelles, sliced, or 15 g / ½ oz / ¼ cup dried, soaked for 20 minutes in warm water
10 ml / 2 tsp almond butter
150 ml / ¼ pint / ⅔ cup crème fraîche
a little milk or water
75 ml / 5 tbsp chopped fresh parsley
50 g / 2 oz / ½ cup grated Parmesan cheese

Cook's Tip
If planning ahead, gnocchi can be shaped ready for cooking up to 8 hours in advance. Almond butter is available ready-made from health food shops.

1 Cover the potatoes with cold salted water, bring to the boil and cook for 20 minutes. Drain and set aside. Place the pumpkin in a bowl, cover and microwave on full power for 8 minutes. Alternatively, wrap the pumpkin in foil and bake at 180°C / 350°F / Gas 4 for 30 minutes. Drain well then add to the potato and pass through a vegetable mill into a bowl. Add the egg yolks, flour, spices, orange rind and seasoning and mix well to make a soft dough. Add more flour if the mixture is too loose.

2 Bring a large pan of salted water to the boil, then dredge a work surface with plain flour. Spoon the gnocchi mixture into a piping bag fitted with a 1 cm / ½ in plain nozzle. Pipe onto the floured surface to make a 15 cm / 6 in sausage. Roll in flour and cut into 2.5 cm / 1 in pieces. Repeat the process making more sausage shapes. Mark each lightly with a fork and cook for 3–4 minutes in the boiling water.

3 Meanwhile, make the sauce. Heat the oil in a non-stick frying pan, add the shallot and fry until soft without colouring. Add the chanterelles and cook briefly, then add the almond butter. Stir to melt and stir in the crème fraîche. Simmer briefly and adjust the consistency with milk or water. Add the parsley and season to taste.

4 Lift the gnocchi out of the water with a slotted spoon, turn into bowls and spoon the sauce over the top. Scatter with Parmesan cheese.

Creamy Beetroot and Potato Gratin with Wild Mushrooms

Polish communities make the most of robust flavours in their cooking and are often first in the woods when mushrooms appear. This inexpensive dish captures the spirit of their autumn menus.

SERVES 4

30 ml / 2 tbsp vegetable oil

1 medium onion, chopped

45 ml / 3 tbsp plain flour

300 ml / ½ pint / 1¼ cups vegetable stock

675 g / 1½ lb cooked beetroot, peeled and chopped

75 ml / 5 tbsp single cream

30 ml / 2 tbsp creamed horseradish

5 ml / 1 tsp hot mustard

15 ml / 1 tbsp wine vinegar

5 ml / 1 tsp caraway seeds

25 g / 1 oz / 2 tbsp unsalted butter

1 shallot, chopped

225 g / 8 oz assorted wild and cultivated mushrooms such as ceps, bay boletus, chanterelles, chicken of the woods, blewits, fairy ring, parasol, oyster, field, shiitake, St George's and Caesar's mushrooms, trimmed and sliced

45 ml / 3 tbsp chopped fresh parsley

For the Potato Border

900 g / 2 lb floury potatoes, peeled

150 ml / ¼ pint / ⅔ cup milk

15 ml / 1 tbsp chopped fresh dill (optional)

salt and freshly ground black pepper

1 Preheat the oven to 190°C / 375°F / Gas 5. Lightly oil a 23 cm / 9 in round baking dish. Heat the oil in a large saucepan, add the onion and fry until soft without colouring. Stir in the flour, remove from the heat and gradually add the stock, stirring until well blended.

2 Return to the heat, stir and simmer to thicken, then add the beetroot, cream, creamed horseradish, mustard, vinegar and caraway seeds.

3 Bring the potatoes to the boil in salted water and cook for 20 minutes. Drain well and mash with the milk. Add the dill if using and season to taste with salt and pepper.

4 Spoon the potatoes into the prepared dish and make a well in the centre. Spoon the beetroot mixture into the well and set aside.

5 Melt the butter in a large non-stick frying pan and fry the shallot until soft, without browning. Add the mushrooms and cook over a moderate heat until their juices begin to run. Increase the heat and boil off the moisture. When quite dry, season and stir in the chopped parsley. Spread the mushrooms over the beetroot mixture, cover and bake for 30 minutes.

Cook's Tip

If planning ahead, this entire dish can be made in advance and heated through when needed. Allow 50 minutes baking time from room temperature.

Kedgeree of Oyster and Chanterelle Mushrooms

Providing breakfast for an army of late risers is quite a challenge. This delicious kedgeree combines the rich woodland flavour of oyster and chanterelle mushrooms with eggs, rice and a touch of curry seasoning.

SERVES 4

- *250g / 1 oz / 2 tbsp butter*
- *1 medium onion, chopped*
- *400g / 14 oz / 2 cups long grain rice*
- *1 small carrot, cut into julienne strips*
- *900 ml / 1½ pints / 3¾ cups vegetable stock, boiling*
- *1 pinch saffron*
- *225g / 8 oz oyster and chanterelle mushrooms, trimmed and halved*
- *115g / 4 oz floury potato, peeled and grated*
- *450 ml / ¾ pint / 1⅞ cup milk*
- *½ vegetable stock cube*
- *2.5 ml / ½ tsp curry paste*
- *30 ml / 2 tbsp double cream*
- *4 eggs*
- *60 ml / 4 tbsp chopped fresh parsley*

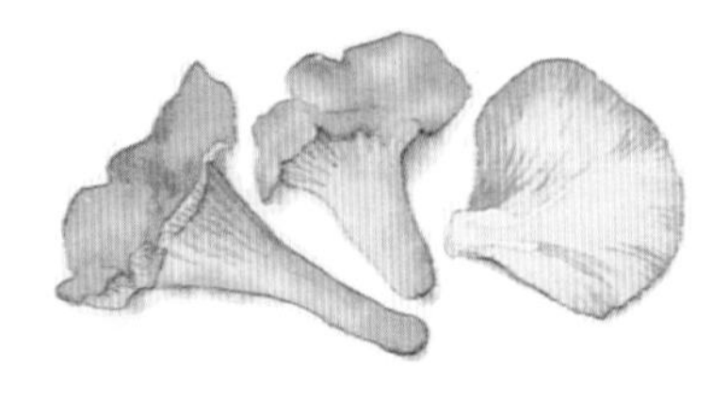

Cook's Tip
Kedgeree will keep warm without spoiling in a covered dish for up to 2 hours.

1 Melt the butter in a large saucepan, add the onion and fry it gently without letting it colour.

2 Turn half of the softened onion into a medium-sized saucepan. Put the rice, carrot and stock in the large pan, add a pinch of saffron, stir and simmer, uncovered for 15 minutes. Remove the pan from the heat, cover and stand for 5 minutes.

3 Add the oyster and chanterelle mushrooms to the pan with the onion and cook gently for a few minutes to soften. Add the grated potato, milk, stock cube and curry paste and simmer for 15 minutes until the potatoes have thickened the liquid.

4 Place the eggs in a pan of boiling water and cook for 10 minutes. Run them under cold water to cool, then peel and cut into quarters.

5 Fork the rice onto a warmed serving platter. Spoon the mushrooms and sauce into the centre and garnish with the egg quarters and chopped parsley.

Cook's Tip
There are many varieties of long grain rice available. The least flavoursome are the non-stick brands that have been part cooked to remove a proportion of starch. The notion that every grain of rice must be separate undermines the nature and flavour of good rice.

Mushroom Boreg

The Turkish boreg or *börek* is a rich pastry parcel with a savoury filling.

SERVES 4

50 g / 2 oz / ⅓ cup couscous
45 ml / 3 tbsp olive oil
1 medium onion, chopped
225 g / 8 oz assorted wild and cultivated mushrooms such as ceps, bay boletus, chanterelles, winter chanterelles, oyster, field, St George's and Caesar's mushrooms, trimmed and sliced
1 garlic clove, crushed
60 ml / 4 tbsp chopped fresh parsley
5 ml / 1 tsp chopped fresh thyme
1 egg, hard-boiled and peeled
salt and freshly ground black pepper

For the Boreg Pastry

400 g / 14 oz / 3½ cups self-raising flour
5 ml / 1 tsp salt
1 egg, plus extra for glazing
150 ml / ¼ pint / ⅔ cup natural yogurt
150 ml / ¼ pint / ⅔ cup olive oil
grated rind of ½ lemon

For the Yogurt Sauce

200 ml / 7 fl oz / ⅞ cup natural yogurt
45 ml / 3 tbsp chopped fresh mint
2.5 ml / ½ tsp caster sugar
1.5 ml / ¼ tsp cayenne pepper
1.5 ml / ¼ tsp celery salt
a little milk or water

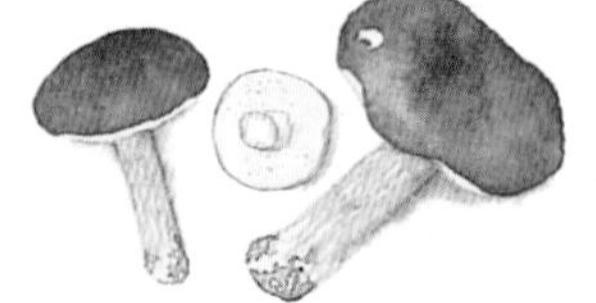

1 Preheat the oven to 190°C / 375°F / Gas 5. Just cover the couscous with boiling water and soak for 10 minutes or until the liquid is absorbed. Then soften the onion in oil without letting it colour. Add the mushrooms and garlic and cook until the juices begin to run, then increase the heat to eliminate the juices. Transfer to a bowl, add the parsley, thyme and couscous and stir well. Grate the hard-boiled egg into the mixture, season and combine.

2 To make the pastry, sift the flour and salt into a bowl. Make a well, add the egg, yogurt, olive oil and lemon rind and combine with a knife.

3 Turn out onto a floured surface and roll into a 30 cm / 12 in circle. Pile the mixture into the centre of the pastry, and bring the edges over, to enclose the filling. Turn upside down onto a baking sheet. Press the boreg out flat with your hand, glaze with beaten egg and bake for 25 minutes.

4 To make the sauce, blend the yogurt with the mint, sugar, cayenne pepper and celery salt, adjusting the consistency with milk or water. Serve boreg at room temperature.

Eggy Rice Cakes with Soured Cream and Mushrooms

SERVES 4

1 egg
15 ml / 1 tbsp plain flour
60 ml / 4 tbsp freshly grated Parmesan, Fontina or Pecorino cheese
400 g / 14 oz / 2 cups cooked long grain rice
salt and freshly ground black pepper
50 g / 2 oz / 4 tbsp unsalted butter, plus extra for frying
1 shallot or small onion, chopped
175 g / 6 oz assorted wild and cultivated mushrooms such as ceps, bay boletus, chanterelles, winter chanterelles, horn of plenty, blewits, field and oyster mushrooms, trimmed and sliced
1 sprig thyme
30 ml / 2 tbsp Madeira or sherry
150 ml / ¼ pint / ⅔ cup soured cream or crème fraîche
paprika for dusting (optional)

1 Beat the egg, flour and cheese together with a fork, then stir in the cooked rice. Mix well and set aside.

2 Fry the shallot or onion in half the butter until soft but not brown. Add the mushrooms and thyme and cook until the juices run. Add the Madeira or sherry. Increase the heat to reduce the juices and concentrate the flavour. Season to taste, transfer to a bowl, cover and keep warm.

3 Fry heaps of the rice mixture in a knob of butter. Cook each one for a minute on each side. When all the rice cakes are cooked, arrange on four warmed plates, top with soured cream or crème fraîche and a spoonful of mushrooms. Dust with paprika and serve with asparagus and baby carrots.

Wild Mushroom Gratin with Beaufort Cheese, New Potatoes, Pickles and Walnuts

This gratin is one of the simplest and most delicious ways of cooking mushrooms. The dish is inspired by the Swiss custom of eating alpine cheeses with new potatoes and small gherkins.

SERVES 4

900 g / 2 lb new potatoes, scrubbed or scraped

50 g / 2 oz / 4 tbsp unsalted butter or 60 ml / 4 tbsp olive oil

350 g / 12 oz assorted wild and cultivated mushrooms such as oyster, shiitake and closed field mushrooms, ceps, bay boletus, chanterelles, winter chanterelles, hedgehog fungus, St George's mushrooms and saffron milk-caps

salt and freshly ground black pepper

175 g / 6 oz Beaufort or Fontina cheese

50 g / 2 oz / ½ cup broken walnuts, toasted

12 medium gherkins and mixed green salad leaves, to serve

1 Place the potatoes in a pan of salted water, bring to the boil and cook for 20 minutes. Drain, add the knob of the butter, cover and keep warm.

2 Trim the mushrooms and then slice them thinly.

3 Fry the mushrooms in the remaining butter or oil. When the juices appear, increase the heat to evaporate the moisture.

4 Preheat a moderate grill. Slice the cheese thinly, arrange on top of the mushroom slices and grill until bubbly and brown. Scatter with walnuts and serve with buttered new potatoes, gherkins and a green salad.

Cook's Tip

For best results, choose an attractive flameproof dish that can be put under the grill and brought directly to the table.

Hash Brown Chicken of the Woods with Potatoes and Onions

The hash brown dinner can range from a welcome treat to a greasy ruin. This recipe calls for the intriguing *Laetiporus sulphureus*, or chicken of the woods, which looks, tastes and has the texture of chicken.

SERVES 4

900 g / 2 lb potatoes, peeled
50 g / 2 oz / 4 tbsp unsalted butter
2 medium onions, sliced
1 celery stick, sliced
1 small carrot, peeled and cut into short batons
225 g / 8 oz chicken of the woods, trimmed and sliced
45 ml / 3 tbsp medium sherry
45 ml / 3 tbsp chopped fresh parsley
15 ml / 1 tbsp chopped fresh chives
grated rind of ½ lemon
salt and freshly ground black pepper

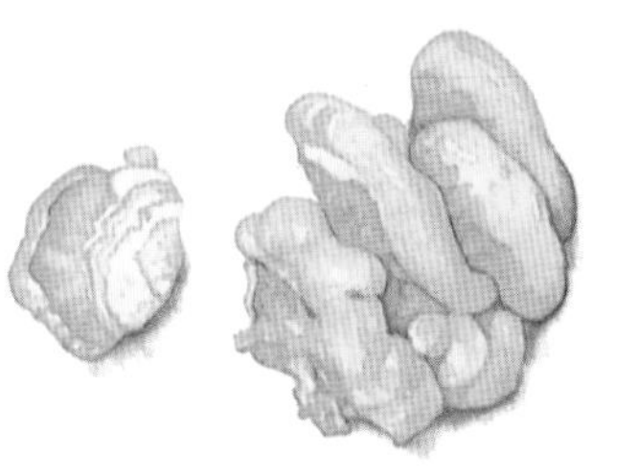

Cook's Tip
The best hash browns are made from late season floury potatoes that are inclined to fall apart when cooked. This quality helps the mixture to form a more solid mass in the pan.

1 Place the potatoes in a saucepan of salted water, bring to the boil and cook for 20 minutes. Drain, cool and slice thickly.

2 Melt the butter in a large non-stick frying pan, add the onions, celery and carrot and fry until lightly browned.

3 Add the chicken of the woods and the sherry, then simmer to evaporate any moisture.

4 Add the potatoes, herbs, lemon rind and seasoning, toss and fry together until crispy brown. Serve with a salad of frisée and young spinach leaves.

Index